T0209853

Winks from God

Linking Life and Prayer

Lesli' S. Downs

WESTBOW
P R E S S®
A DIVISION OF THOMAS NELSON
& ZONDERVAN

WestBow Press books may be ordered through booksellers or by contacting:

WestBow Press
A Division of Thomas Nelson & Zondervan
1663 Liberty Drive
Bloomington, IN 47403
www.westbowpress.com
844-714-3454

Interior Image Credit: Lesli Downs and Chris Baker
Editor: Holly Defatta

ISBN: 978-1-6642-4075-9 (sc)
ISBN: 978-1-6642-4076-6 (hc)
ISBN: 978-1-6642-4074-2 (e)

Library of Congress Control Number: 2021914365

Print information available on the last page.

WestBow Press rev. date: 08/12/2021

I want to give a special thanks to my husband because he believed in what God was doing and he kept me grounded and focused. I love you Kyle and I can't express how much gratitude I have because you helped me see what God placed inside of me and kept me going.

I also want to thank a tribe of women who have surrounded me with prayer, encouragement and helped flourish me. You truly don't figure out who you are until you find your tribe. Once you do, hold on to them because they are there to help you flourish into who God meant for you to be!

Father, thank You for this journey and the tribe of people you placed around me to encourage and flourish me. Amen.

Contents

Bridges

I had a dream last year where several people in armor, including myself, were standing in a gap, and this gap was filled with stones that had words written them. The words were *division, rebellion, malice, slander, lies, hate* and *strongholds*. We were building a bridge to reestablish unity by filling in the gap and helping people cross over to a strong foundation. The building of the bridge began to unify us as one body in Christ, and it helped to mature and season our intercession for our brothers and sisters. This was an old bridge made of square natural stones with mortar between them, and on each stone was written the words above. Once we stacked the stones and sealed them with the mortar, the words would change. It looked like a perfectly aligned assembly line that moved in one swift motion. After each brick was stacked and sealed, you could feel the Lord's mercy coming forth, and the words changed to *love, mercy, faith, hope, grace, trust, righteousness, forgiveness,* and *salvation.* These were the building stones (blocks) that made a strong bridge to support people so that they would trust the bridge they were crossing to rebuild a strong foundation.

> For we are God's fellow workers. You are God's field, God's building. According to the grace of God given to me, like a skilled master builder I laid a foundation, and someone else is building upon it. Let each one take care how he builds upon it. For no one can lay a foundation other than that which is laid, which is Jesus Christ. (1 Corinthians 3:9–11 ESV)

Father, thank You for Your cornerstone, Jesus Christ. Thank You for Your Word that is our foundation. We are in a building season, and we need the blocks to help build Your church. You have already placed these building blocks inside us as gifts. But we doubt and have mistrust in ourselves and our gifts. Father, forgive us for doubting and downgrading our gifts. Lord, tune our senses to see Your movement, and build our trust within us to use these gifts. Help us use these gifts to obtain wisdom, meekness, humility, and courage to stand strong and not remain silent when we should speak and to be silent when we shouldn't speak. Help us to come together in unity to create one body in Christ and bring forth Your glory. Strengthen our shoulders to support and lift those who have fallen into this gap of division! Raise us up as bridges to help all Your lost children cross over to a strong foundation. Help us build and battle while we repair and fill this gap. Lord, I ask if we fall, let us fall together so that we will rise together stronger as one body in Christ. In Yeshua's (Yeshua is the Hebrew name of Jesus) name I pray, Amen!

REFLECTION POINTS:

This week, reflect on what gifts you can offer others to show love and kindness. Then find a way to use those gifts to build trust with someone you don't know well or rebuild trust that may have been lost. It can be something as simple as saying hi and asking how they are, giving them a compliment, paying for lunch, or treating them to their favorite coffee or drink. Small acts of kindness show you listen, and you pay attention to what is going on in others' lives. These are small steps to building trust and sharing love and kindness. At the end of the week, take inventory of your week and look at the areas that you stepped up in and the areas in which you may have missed an opportunity. Make note on how to avoid missing those opportunities again. Then ask God to help you see all the areas of gifts He wants you to step into, and who He wants you to build trust with for His kingdom.

Gullible

I have been seeing seagulls everywhere and in places I don't normally see them. So, I researched seagulls and read more about them. I found they are versatile birds, very adaptable, and good scavengers for food sources. They are known for swallowing almost anything. But what caught my attention was the word *gull*. I am reminded of the word *gullible*. I believe this really says a lot about the world we are in right now. Are we like the seagulls, and do we swallow everything we see or hear? Are we gullible, or do we discern beyond what we see and hear? Let's use the seagull as an example to try not to swallow everything we hear and see. Let's try to step out from the realm of what we see, look beyond what is in front of us, and discern what God is doing! Hebrews 11 shows how faith helps build the foundation God needed to be able to bring forth His promises. Even though many did not see them, they believed in them.

> Now faith brings our hopes into reality and becomes the foundation needed to acquire the things we long for. It is all the evidence required to prove what is still unseen. This testimony of faith is what previous generations were commended for. Faith empowers us to see that the universe was created and beautifully coordinated by the power of God's words! He spoke and the invisible realm gave birth to all that is seen. (Hebrews 11:1–3 TPT)

Father, thank You for the generations that sacrificed to build the foundation we need to stand on. Lord, help us to see the building blocks it takes to bring Your kingdom to earth. No matter what darkness and dim light may surround us, help us to stand firm on Your Word, trust that you have everything perfectly balanced and measured, and know that only you understand the purposes and plans for these building blocks. Lord, many need a heart shock to bring them back to You and open their eyes to see beyond what is in front them. Despite the confusion and aggravation, help us look to the heavens and not rely on our own sight. Help build our faith just like Abraham to see that Your promises will come forth in Your perfect time. Lord, reveal to Your children today how Your love is reckless and how You will tear everything down to get Your love to Your children. Bring heaven and earth into alignment. In Yeshua's name I pray, Amen!

Reflection Points:

No matter what you hear this week, I want to challenge you to take it to prayer and ask God what He says. Get His opinion first, and then form yours around what He said. Then get His written Word out and find the truth. When you choose to listen to God and then formulate what you believe based on what He said, you are walking in God's will. Doing this will sharpen your discernment and will help you to decipher truth from lies. At the end of the week, make note of when you had to take these steps to see the truth. Was there a verse that you read that really helped you see that truth? Refer back to that verse when you need reassurance.

Time

It seems like things take so long to happen, but at the same time, days are going so fast. This period of waiting for something to happen and time flying by, feels like a place of limbo.

> But do not overlook this one fact, beloved, that with the Lord one day is as a thousand years, and a thousand years as one day. The Lord is not slow to fulfill his promise as some count slowness, but is patient toward you, not wishing that any should perish, but that all should reach repentance. (2 Peter 3:8–9 ESV)

So, the Lord's timing covers a thousand years in one day! Could that be because God already knows our end, and He knows the best timing and way to get to the end?

> Yet God has made everything beautiful for its own time. He has planted eternity in the human heart, but even so, people cannot see the whole scope of God's work from beginning to end. (Ecclesiastes 3:11 NLT)

Limbo is hard to stay in, but I believe God has us all here for a reason. Since He knows the end already, I am going to trust He has a way out and something new is coming.

> And a highway will be there; it will be called the Way of Holiness; it will be for those who walk on that Way...They will enter Zion with singing;

everlasting joy will crown their heads. Gladness and joy will overtake them, and sorrow and sighing will flee away. (Isaiah 35:8–10 NIV)

Amen!

Father, thank You for Your timing! Your timing is perfect and full of love! Lord, help us through limbo. Help us to stretch our minds to see Your timing. Lord, reveal the beauty of Your time and lead us to the highway to everlasting joy! Grow our hearts close to Your heart and unveil eternity to us. Bless us with eyes to see Your time, a heart to be patient with time, and ears to hear when the time is near! May Your kingdom come, and Your will be done here on earth as in heaven. In Yeshua's name I pray, Amen!

REFLECTION POINTS:

I want to give you one challenge this week: sit down with God, read His Word, talk with Him, and forget about time. Turn some worship music on, get a pad of paper and pencil, and get your Bible out. No clocks—that means no phones or watches either. Just sit in His presence and give your time to Him. Write down anything He puts on your heart and meditate on the word He gives you. When you can't see past the timing of things and need encouragement, go back and read it again. Write down any Bible verses that stuck out and lean on His Word.

Keys

I was thinking about heavenly authority while reading Matthew 16:17–19, in which Jesus tells Peter he will be the rock on which Jesus will build His church. He will be given the keys of heaven and the gates of hell won't prevail against it. Isaiah 22:22 also refers to the keys which open and close doors that no one else can. We know Jesus died and rose again with these keys. We read this in Matthew 27:51–54, in which tombs were opened and dead saints walked among the living. Imagine Jesus dying on the cross and the sky darkens for three hours (Luke 23:44–46). What do you think was happening in the spirit world at this moment? His adversary (Satan) is sitting on his throne in hell, laughing and celebrating because he thinks he has won, and around his neck are the keys that can set captives free from their chains! Then all the sudden, Jesus walks up to him and takes the keys away! Imagine his face—how he trembled, and how the authority he thought he had was just taken from him. He knew that authority was given back to the children of God, so we could crush the enemy's head! Fear, lies, corruption, sickness, pestilence, or tragedy cannot knock the gates down or even open them! But Jesus gave us KEYS to lock these doors. Worship, pray and dance to God because He has given us this authority and we should celebrate Him (Revelation 1:17–19)!

> God shall arise, his enemies shall be scattered…. so the wicked shall perish before God! But the righteous shall be glad…exult before God…be jubilant with joy! Sing to God, sing praises to his name; lift up a song to him who rides through the deserts; his name is the Lord; exult before him! (Psalm 68:1–4 ESV)

Lord, thank You for authority! Thank You for Your Son Yeshua! I come today and rejoice because the battle is won! I will dance and sing unto Your Holy name! I will blow my shofar and declare the enemy is crushed! I will rattle my tambourine and march upon his head, for You have the victory, Lord! Show us the keys to build our temple and fortify our gates, so the enemy cannot prevail! Bring heaven and earth into alignment! In Yeshua's name I pray, Amen!

REFLECTION POINTS:

This week prepare yourself every morning by positioning your heart towards God and worshipping Him. Find a song that makes you feel like a warrior and begin to fight with your worship! I personally like the song by We the Kingdom "Don't Tread on Me".

It reminds me who I am—a child of the King with kingdom authority. With that authority, Jesus gave me the keys to lock the gates of hell so they will not prevail! Those powerful keys are the Word of God!

Transformation

Resist him, firm in your faith, knowing that the same kinds of suffering are being experienced by your brotherhood throughout the world. And after you have suffered a little while, the God of all grace, who has called you to his eternal glory in Christ, will himself restore, confirm, strengthen, and establish you. To him be the dominion forever and ever. Amen. (1 Peter 5:9–11 ESV)

One summer I saw red dragonflies that I had never seen before. They are understood to represent life and death through transformation. When I read that, I thought about the phrase *to die to self.* In Romans 8, it states that to set your mind on the flesh is hostile to God, and the flesh can never please God. This new cycle of life I am in, is tiring and seems to test my character in many ways. I feel like my emotions are everywhere some days. I personally know that my character needed to be tested, because I have become very accustomed to this world and my flesh. In the process, I was very complacent to God, and I needed to get control of my emotions. I looked up the Greek word for character, *ethos.* As I researched, two other words seem to tie in with ethos— *logos* and *pathos.* Ethos is about your character, logos refers to your words, reason, or speech, and pathos is how you use your compassion or emotion to sway people with your ethos and logos. I have decided to *die to self,* let God change my accustomed place to seek His heart and let me see others as He sees them. I took hold of my emotions and asked God to help me see beyond what was in front of me. I want to challenge all of you today to stop and get control of your emotions, die to self, and let God transform you.

Father, thank You for the virtues You planted deep within us. I ask You to come, Lord, and awaken those virtues, and change the accustomed places of all Your children from this world into Your presence. Father, show us how to tap into our abundant supply of gifts from You to seek Your heart! Show us how to use those gifts with our character, our speech, and our compassion, to serve others as Your Son did. Give us a servant's heart like Your Son Jesus Christ, and help us to wash other's feet with compassion and mercy, as He did. Father, transform, restore, confirm, strengthen, and establish us for Your dominion and with Your kingdom authority. Lord, we await heaven's gate to open for our triumphant entrance into Your presence. May Your kingdom come, and Your will be done here on earth as in heaven. In Yeshua's name I pray, Amen!

Reflection Points:

Every morning this week, before you get out of bed, ask God to help you keep control of your emotions and help you discern what God may be teaching you about your character. Make note throughout the week when you were able to accurately discern your situation, keeping emotions out that didn't belong, using emotions to help sharpen your discernment, and how you shifted your *ethos*, *logos*, and *pathos* towards God. Take note of when emotions didn't help your discernment and how to avoid those emotions again.

Salt

You are the salt of the earth, but if salt has lost
its taste, how shall its saltiness be restored? It is
no longer good for anything except to be thrown
out and trampled under people's feet. (Matthew
5:13 ESV)

We had a sermon at church that talked about being the salt of the
earth, and a memory came to mind. When I was in high school, I went
to help a neighbor get organized for a garage sale. While helping her
move things, I noticed she had a cut on her arm, and it looked like she
had poured something grainy on top of it. I asked her what happened.
She replied, "I cut my arm and I poured salt on it." I said, "SALT!
Doesn't that hurt?" She said, "It does hurt, but I know the salt will
purify and clean the wound and it will heal back properly." I remember
thinking this lady doesn't know what she is talking about! But after
I thought about what she said, it made sense. Being a Christian isn't
easy. It isn't easy standing up for what you value and believe in a loving
and respectful way, especially when someone comes along and leaves a
bad taste in your mouth. Be salt that purifies, edifies, and heals with
love and does not divide with hate.

Lord, thank You for being salt and showing us how to be that as
well. Abba Father, it is hard sometimes and it hurts. This world seems
to be filled with bad tasting flavors! Help us to see the path to healing
and purity! Restore us to the pure salt You have called us to be. Help
us to leave a loving, merciful, and bold flavor that speaks Your truth
and brings glory to Your name. In Yeshua's name I pray, Amen!

REFLECTIONS POINTS:

This week, really pay attention to not just how you respond to others that seem to make you close your eyes and sigh, but how others may respond to them. Find a way to be respectful, loving, and kind to them, even though they may not return the favor. God knows, and He is working even in the times it feels like He isn't even there. If it is too hard to take that step, then just pray for them, or as one of my pastors always says just pray for their dog.

Potholes

Yes, God is more than ready to overwhelm you with every form of grace, so that you will have more than enough of everything—every moment and in every way. He will make you overflow with abundance in every good thing you do. (2 Corinthians 9:8 TPT)

I love the song "What If I Stumble" by a group from the 90's called DC Talk. This song talks about walking in God's purpose and trying to be an example of how to do so. But at the same time, it talks about the doubt we all experience, because we believe that we aren't good enough, that we will fall and stumble, and that we fear it. I know for me, when I have stumbled and hurt someone on the way down, the pain of the fall stings a lot more. But I have learned that every misstep, every fall, and every stumble has a purpose and a meaning. Every time God was there wiping my knees off and saying, "Okay, what did you learn?" I learned that He is more than enough to catch you when you fall. When you get back up, He is more than enough to cover the inadequacy you feel for falling. His grace is enough for you to get up, wipe yourself off, and move on. You learned something, and now you can prevent someone else from falling in the same pothole you did!

Lord, thank You for Your grace. Thank You for the living Word and how powerful it truly is. Abba, I come and ask You to cover all of us with grace that conquers over doubt, fear, and the inadequacy we feel when we stumble and fall. With every moment and in every way, overflow Your grace onto our paths so we have an abundance of "more than enough" from You to cover us and keep us on the path that is before us. Father, bless us today with the abundance of Your love to cover us with grace in every way possible. In Yeshua's name we pray, Amen.

REFLECTION POINTS:

This week, more than likely, you may stumble and fall, but know your Father will be there to wipe you off and help you see that pothole that tripped you up. He will teach you how to avoid it and how to help others. Make note of potholes that trip you up, and ask God to help you avoid them, and then help others as well.

It is Well

Who comforteth us in all our tribulation, that we may be able to comfort them which are in any trouble, by the comfort wherewith we ourselves are comforted of God.

(2 Corinthians 1:4 KJV)

The hymn, "It Is Well with My Soul," was written by Horatio Spafford after traumatic events happened in his life, beginning with the death of his four-year-old son, followed by the Great Chicago Fire of 1871, which ruined him financially. Then in 1873, he sent his wife and four daughters to Europe on the *SS Ville du Havre*. While crossing the Atlantic Ocean, the ship sank rapidly and all four of Spafford's daughters died but his wife survived. While Spafford traveled on a ship to meet his grieving wife, he was inspired to write the song as the ship passed near the area where all four of his daughters died. Many have suffered and are still suffering right now. So, I want to give comfort to the many who are suffering and say God will make it well with your soul.

Lord, thank You for Your love, mercy, and grace. It gives us comfort and helps us heal our weary souls. Lord, many are sick in their spirit from all the tragedy that seems to surround and engulf this world right now. Lord, I lift my brothers and sisters up to You and I ask Lord, make it well with their souls! Soothe the pain and hurt. Wrap them in Your love and take their heart and make it new! Mend this tear that this world ripped through their lives. Give them hope again! Lord, bless Your children today with love to fill their hearts, grace that will guide their steps, and hope to make their spirit rise! May Your kingdom come, Your will be done on earth as it is in heaven. In Yeshua's name we pray, Amen!

Reflection Points:

This week, you, or someone you know, may be facing difficult times and may need prayer and encouragement. Ask God to show you how to give comfort to those suffering, and if you are the one suffering, don't isolate yourself away from people. God has already found a way to make it well with your soul, so allow Him to let you be loved and comforted by others.

Walk with You

The Lord is my shepherd; I have all that I need.
He lets me rest in green meadows; he leads me
beside peaceful streams. He renews my strength.
He guides me along the right paths, bringing honor
to his name. Even when I walk through the darkest
valley, I will not be afraid, for you are close beside
me. Your rod and your staff protect and comfort
me. You prepare a feast for me in the presence of my
enemies. You honor me by anointing my head with
oil. My cup overflows with blessings. Surely your
goodness and unfailing love will pursue me all the
days of my life, and I will live in the house of the
Lord forever. (Psalm 23:1–6 NLT)

Walk with You.

Lord, may I walk with You today?
For You are my watcher and my trust is in You.
And in the darkest valleys I know You are beside me.

Do You mind if I step where you step today?
Then I am guided along the right path
and I will honor Your name.

Would You show me Your heart today?
For You are filled with goodness and unfailing love!
And You will pursue me with unbounded love until the end of
my days.

Could I see one of Your dreams for me today?
For I want to see green meadows, peaceful streams,
and the feast of victory You have prepared for me.

If I stumble, do You mind catching my fall?
I know Your rod and staff will protect me
and give me comfort on the way back up.

May I rest in Your arms along the way?
Lord, You are my strength so please anoint my head with Your oil
and overflow my cup with Your blessing today.
For I will live in the house of the Lord forever! Amen!

REFLECTION POINTS:

This week, find time to go and take a walk with God.

Barabas

"But you have a custom of asking me to release one prisoner each year at Passover. Would you like me to release this 'King of the Jews'?" But they shouted back, "No! Not this man. We want Barabbas!" (Barabbas was a revolutionary.) (John 18:39–40 NLT)

I never noticed that the name Barabbas has the word *abba* in it, which means father. It made me curious, and I discovered that the Aramaic meaning for Barabbas is "son of the father." Jesus is also called "son of the father" (2 John 1:3). I tried to imagine myself as Barabbas, "son of the father," and Jesus, "Son of the Father," standing next to each other, watching and waiting for people to chant, "Kill Barabbas!" But they don't! They say kill Jesus! I don't know what I would have done, knowing this sinless "Son of the Father" was going to die for me, a sinful "son of the father!" The Lord loves us that much, to give His Son for us (John 3:16).

Lord, thank You for Your perfect Son, Jesus Christ. Lord, I don't have the words to express how beautiful Your Word is! How everything that surrounds us has a meaning to You, has a purpose for You, and will Glorify Your name. Thank You for saving me by sending Your Son to exchange His life for mine and setting me free! I surrender my life completely to You, Lord, for it is the least I could do! Bless your Son, Jesus Christ! Lord, bless us with grace, mercy, and peace today. In Yeshua's name we pray, Amen.

Reflection Points:

No matter where you are in your walk with God, remember, there is nothing His Son, Jesus Christ, didn't take to the cross and that His blood won't cover. Your salvation through Jesus Christ covers all past, present and future sins and no sin is too great for Him to forgive. He will forgive you if you forgive others, so this week, receive God's forgiveness for your sins and forgive others of theirs as Christ did for you.

Wedding Day

For you reach into my heart. With one flash of your eyes I am undone by your love, my beloved, my equal, my bride. You leave me breathless— I am overcome by merely a glance from your worshiping eyes, for you have stolen my heart. I am held hostage by your love and by the graces of righteousness shining upon you. (Song of Songs 4:9 TPT)

Do you remember your wedding day? All the preparation and effort required to make everything perfect! Waiting to walk down the aisle and say I do. Recall the butterflies, the overwhelming uncontrollable emotions, and your spouse's eyes when you see each other at the altar. For a moment, close your eyes and picture that day, even if it hasn't come yet. What does it look like? Now walk down the aisle, look at the altar, and picture Jesus standing there waiting to make you His bride! As you exchange vows, the verse above is what Jesus says to you. When you feel like love is gone, your trust is undone, and you're so angry at everything around you, close your eyes and picture that altar with Jesus standing there! Let His love wrap you up and give you rest!

Lord, thank You for this love that we don't deserve! Lord, I ask only one thing today. Bless Your children with love today. Wrap Your love tightly around Your children and give them rest.

In Yeshua's name we pray, Amen!

REFLECTION POINTS:

This week at lunch, say a quick prayer before you eat, and ask God to help you prepare to be the bride of Christ, and to wrap you in His love along the way.

Olive Press

"Father, if you are willing, please take this cup of suffering away from me. Yet I want your will to be done, not mine." Then an angel from heaven appeared and strengthened him. He prayed more fervently, and he was in such agony of spirit that his sweat fell to the ground like great drops of blood. (Luke 22:42–44 NLT)

Did you know the name Christ comes from a Greek word meaning *anointed one, to anoint, or one who is anointed*? The name Gethsemane comes from a Hebrew word meaning *oil press*. While Jesus was praying in the garden, He was being pressed. As His sweat fell to the ground "like drops of blood" (Luke 22:44), He felt His spirit being crushed by the burdens of all our sins and by the weight of the Father's will.

But he was pierced for our transgressions; he was crushed for our iniquities; upon him was the chastisement that brought us peace, and with his wounds we are healed. (Isaiah 53:5 ESV)

Yeshua's anointing not only brings us peace, but healing. So today, celebrate Yeshua because He was crushed for His anointing to cover us with peace and heal our wounds.

Lord, thank You for the anointing You placed on Your Son, and that He was pressed for us to be anointed with peace and healing! Today, I ask for Your anointing to cover us from head to toe and provide peace and healing. As Your anointing flows, let Your presence dwell within us overflow onto others. Lord, bring revival and pour Your anointing out on this nation and all Your children today. In Yeshua's name we pray, Amen.

REFLECTION POINTS:

Every day this week, thank God for His Son and the anointing He has given to you. Ask Him to help you walk within that anointing to fulfill His glory.

#ACTS

Acts

"Go therefore and make disciples of all nations, baptizing them in the name of the Father and of the Son and of the Holy Spirit, teaching them to observe all that I have commanded you. And behold, I am with you always, to the end of the age." (Matthew 28:19–20 ESV)

The best offense is a good defense! For some reason, this phrase has been replaying over and over in my mind, and I have been trying to figure out what that looks like in daily life. I was reading the book of Acts in The Apologetics Study Bible, and the first line in the introduction to the book of Acts stated that "Acts bridged the gap between the four gospel accounts and the Epistles that follow." An image flashed in my mind of small groups, churches, and a picture of life outside these areas. After reading the bold offensive stance the twelve apostles took against the world, and their courageous defending stance towards Jesus, I realized, this is the foundation that we still should stand on today (Matthew 28:18-20). So, I started to picture church service as practice. The place where we come together as one body in Christ to worship, to get direction, and to sharpen our skills. Similarly, small groups are huddles in the middle of the game to gather and regroup, to encourage, to motivate and to lean on each other for the strategies and plans for this game of life. The main goal for Christians isn't just about getting saved, it is about teaching people how to live a Christian life and knowing how to apply the Word to all aspects of life, even in the most practical ways. Just like the acts of the apostles were challenging and hard, so will ours be, but we learn to lean on our teammates in the body of Christ to help us through the challenges, just as they did (Acts 4). This is how we learn to strengthen our defense, by standing in unity through our offense.

Father, thank You for alignment and how You use church and small groups to help align Your children into the body of Christ. Position us to be bridges that build trust with our actions and help us disciple nations by sharing Your truth. Give us game time strategies to build a strong defense against Satan and help us sharpen ourselves and learn how to use our teammates effectively to unify our offense. Guide each of our steps with discernment and authority, and help us to use our actions to bridge the gaps caused by the lies and mistrust from the enemy. Bless all Your children with a revived heart of fire. In Yeshua's name we pray, Amen.

Reflection Points:

This week, join a church, small group, or prayer group and start sharpening your skills, as well as being a sharpening tool for others. I challenge you to be brave and take that step to help further the kingdom of God!

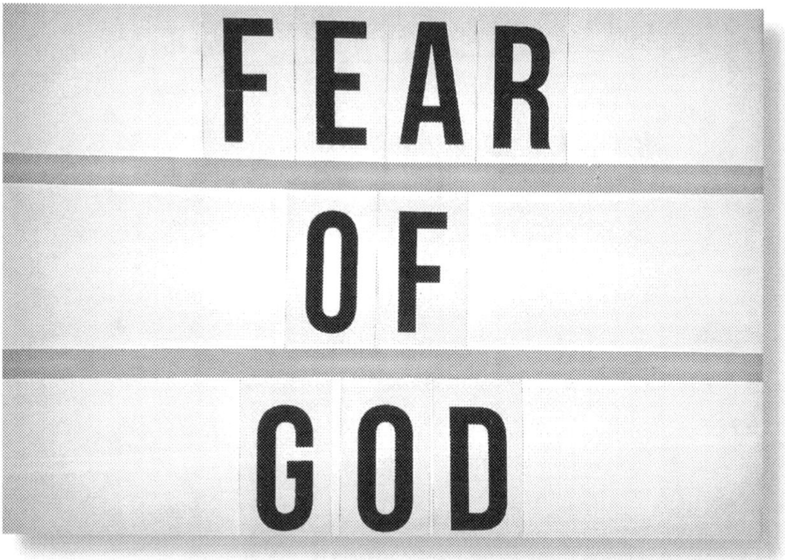
FEAR
OF
GOD

Fear of God

And I saw what appeared to be a sea of glass mingled with fire—and also those who had conquered the beast and its image and the number of its name, standing beside the sea of glass with harps of God in their hands. And they sing the song of Moses, the servant of God, and the song of the Lamb, saying, "Great and amazing are your deeds, O Lord God the Almighty! Just and true are your ways, O King of the nations! Who will not fear, O Lord, and glorify your name? For you alone are holy. All nations will come and worship you, for your righteous acts have been revealed." (Revelation 15:2–4 ESV)

In February 2021, we had a week of incredible weather, our nation seemed so divided, and many people in big ministries fell. As a result, I was shaken. I began to pray and ask God what was going on. He reminded me of a dream I have shared to a few people. In it, I was walking through the desert with a mirror and a cobra strikes the mirror two times. I repositioned my stance to stand strong before the strike, and the shadow of the mirror was protecting me, not only from the heat of the sun, but also the strike of the cobra. Over and over one week, God kept highlighting snakes and the rattling or shaking of the mirror. Even during church one day, our pastor used a rattle trap lure for an illustration. Okay, I knew God was telling me something. I started thinking about everything that is going on and praying more. While I was reading the last chapters of Job, starting in chapter 39, I was reminded of the fear of the Lord. He reminds Job of what He created and how powerful and all knowing He is! He tells Job, "Whatever is under the whole heaven is mine." (Job 41:11 ESV) Even as I read these last chapters, I could feel that fear. I felt God was showing me that His fear is coming, and those who are positioned with a strong stance under the protection of His shadow will not be rattled by God's fear. They will be overwhelmed by how mighty He is and the knowledge He will bring. However, the light He will reflect off the mirror will rattle others who are not under the protection of His shadow. I encourage you to read the last few chapters of Job and see if you feel the fear of God.

Father, thank You for Your mighty power and Your fear that will bring everyone to their knees singing Holy, Holy, is the Lord Almighty! Lord, I ask for forgiveness and mercy to flow on everyone who is not under the protection of Your shadow. Father, show us how to position our stance and give us the tools to battle for the hearts who are lost, confused, and hardened. Help us to brace for the rattle that is coming, to see where the true battles are, and not to be distracted by man's battles! Father, it is time for us to be Biblically correct and stop being politically correct! Lord, show us how to shatter this image that the cobra is reflecting into this world. Show us how we, as the body of Christ, should reflect Your image so others see they are image bearers of You, created in Your image! Bless us with revelation and wisdom to stand strong and battle together. Thank You for Your protection, grace, mercy, and this rattling coming forth. May Your will be done on earth as in heaven. In Yeshua's name I pray, Amen.

REFLECTION POINTS:

This week, pay close attention to people around you, and lift them up in prayer. Pray God uses you to help them see the protection of God and help them trust in God's protection. Pray God gives you grace, mercy, compassion, and wisdom to help others see His image.

#IMAGE
BEARER

Image Bearer

Yet we don't see ourselves as capable enough to do anything in our own strength, for our true competence flows from God's empowering presence. (2 Corinthians 3:5 TPT)

One day a hummingbird came and sat on my olive tree, and I began to research these remarkable little birds. I was amazed how they hover to eat. With each complete beat of their wings, it makes a figure eight pattern. The wings are like swivels which can go up and down, when hovering, and back and forth when flying. God made the hummingbird to display evidence of His careful and loving design for its remarkable lifestyle. If He took such loving care in the design of such a small creature, what kind of love and care do you think He put into you? You were designed in His image after all.

Lord, thank You for Your wonder and the careful details You have put into all Your creatures. I know if You put so much loving detail and care into Your creation, then You put even more into the children You created in Your own image. Lord, show all Your children that You see them as wonders! Strengthen them and encourage them to see You as their reflection. Help them to see they can do all things through You, and that the capabilities You placed in them, are beyond what they can see! Bless all Your children today with Your presence and fill their hearts with Your loving grace. Empower them to see what You see in them! May Your will be done on earth as in heaven. In Yeshua's name we pray, Amen!

Reflection Points:

> So God created man in his own image, in the image
> of God he created him; male and female he created
> them. (Genesis 1:27 ESV)

Every day this week, read this verse and remind yourself who you are—an image bearer. Every day write something positive about yourself and ask Him to help you see how to use that for His kingdom and glory. Then, thank God for creating you and placing you in such a time as this.

Pride

When pride comes, then comes disgrace, but with the humble is wisdom. (Proverbs 11:2 ESV)

And God said, "This is the sign of the covenant that I make between me and you and every living creature that is with you, for all future generations: I have set my bow in the cloud, and it shall be a sign of the covenant between me and the earth." (Genesis 9:12–13 ESV)

I was sitting in the left-hand turn lane one day behind a truck that had a rainbow sticker with the word *pride* on it. The light changes and this truck turns, but is mistakenly driving on the wrong side of the median. I had a car in the lane next to me that followed this truck, and I had followed the truck in order for this car not to hit me. The man next to me realized what he was doing before we passed the median, but the truck didn't. Luckily, it was able to drive over the median before getting hit. In the Bible, the rainbow is a sign of hope and humility, not pride and carelessness. We must be careful which rainbow we follow because you can be pulled down the wrong side and get hit head on!

Lord, thank You for the covenant You have placed between every living creature including us. Thank you for the rainbow as the sign that you are a merciful and loving God. Lord, pride is shifty and sometimes hidden! I ask You today to expose any pride I have hidden in my heart. Forgive me of pride and disgrace! Lord, lead me to humility and wisdom. I lift all my brothers and sisters up and ask for intercession on their behalf for forgiveness of any hidden pride they may have. Reveal pride to us and take it out. Replace it with humility and Your love. May Your will be done on earth as in heaven. In the name of Yeshua I pray, Amen!

REFLECTION POINTS:

This week, ask God to check your heart before you leave your house, and ask Him to show you if any pride is hidden within your heart and to remove it. Make note of any day God speaks to you and checks your heart.

#IAM

I AM

And God said unto Moses, I AM THAT I AM: and he said, Thus shalt thou say unto the children of Israel, I AM hath sent me unto you. (Exodus 3:14 KJV)

So God created man in his own image, in the image of God he created him; male and female he created them. (Genesis 1:27 ESV)

If anyone destroys God's temple, God will destroy him. For God's temple is holy, and you are that temple. (1 Corinthians 3:17 ESV)

When God says, "I AM THAT I AM," it is really mind blowing to me. I realize that because God created us and lives in us, He is I AM to us. Our identity as children of God is so closely weaved to Him, that when you tell someone your name you say "I am" first. If you are going to do something you say "I am" first. If you are going through something you say "I am" first. He is the "I am" that goes with you always. He is the "I am" that created you in His image. He is the "I am" that will never leave you. When you say, "I am," remember that God is with you and dwells inside you. He knows your story because He wrote your story and knows the end from the beginning and the details in the middle. Trust Him, and know I AM has already walked before you.

Lord, thank You for being "I AM"! You are all there was, all there is now, and all there is to come! Lord, awaken our hearts to this great understanding, that we are a part of "I AM" and You will never leave us or forsake us. Show us how to be coworkers with You, and how to help You build Your temple. The great "I AM," I ask You today to bless Your children with Your presence, so they feel that connection with You when they say "I am." May your will be done on earth as in heaven. In Yeshua's name I pray, Amen!

Reflection Points:

Before you do anything this week, ask God to go before you and prepare the way. Take each step knowing that it was already placed there for you to step into.

#UNRAVEL

Unravel

> Then Elijah said to all the people, "Come near to me." And all the people came near to him. And he repaired the altar of the Lord that had been thrown down. (1 Kings 18:30 ESV)

Sometimes I get stuck on one verse for weeks, or one song that I play on repeat over and over.

I have been thinking about 1 Kings 18:30 for a while. Elijah asks the people to "come near to me." And all the people came near to him. Then he took 12 stones and repaired the altar. Elijah's name means Yahweh is God. When he asks them to come near to himself, he is saying come near to Yahweh your God and let Him repair your altar. Altars are places where we separate ourselves to God, and where the natural and supernatural converge. Altars represent a place to be filled with God's presence. There you can reconcile your relationship with God by remembering His loving kindness, ask for mercy to repair your broken heart, and begin to see God's will for your life. Before revival can come, we must be brought back to life and be restored, so the presence of God can come and dwell at our altar and pour mercy on us. I began to ask God how to repair my altar. His answer came through a song I have been listening to over and over lately— "Unraveling" by Cory Asbury. Before I can fix my altar, I must be unraveled from this world, so God's presence can collide with my reality and overtake it with His kingdom to fulfill His will in my life.

Father, thank You for the unmerited, gracious, and loving mercy You pour over us. Abba, please come into my dwelling and unravel the whole thing! Rebuild me at the altar where Your mercy will cover me, and Your love will fill me. Father, converge Your presence with my reality, overtake it with Your kingdom, and fulfill Your will in my life. I want to lift all my brothers and sisters to You. I ask You to overtake them with Your presence, lead them back to the altar, unravel this world from them, and mend them to You. In Yeshua's name I pray, Amen!

REFLECTIONS POINTS:

Listen to "Unraveling" by Cory Asbury throughout the week when you are alone driving in your car, or when you have a moment alone. Surrender all your worship to God and let Him unravel this world from you.

Ten Doors

I have been having a recurring dream I want to share. In the dream, there was a hallway with five doors perfectly aligned on each side, ten doors total. On the left side, the doors were open, and people were walking around who looked tired, weary, and had no color. They were walking in and out of the hallway. Suddenly, the doors on the right side opened, and many people began to walk through the doors on the right but did not come back through. Then, I could hear this loud roaring noise coming down the hall. It was a wave of fire on the left and a wave of water on the right, rolling down side by side. As it came, the doors on the left slammed shut, but the doors on the right remained open. As the wave came, the doors on the left were burned to a crisp, sealed up, and didn't even look like doors anymore. On the right side, the water rushed through the doors, and all the people who had walked through were covered from head to toe. They were revived and illuminated with color! But there were people who were on the left side that never stepped through the open doors (Malachi 1:10–14). The number five is associated with grace, prayers, anointing, maturity, unity, authority, purpose, and will. The number ten symbolizes the authority of God, His government on the Earth, and the responsibility of people towards God's law. God's fire is going to burn you or refine you by purifying you (Luke 3:16–17). Satan wants to take advantage of our natural circumstances, and uses our temper, state of health, and emotions to plague and overwhelm us. More often, we are driven into the fire of presumption or the waters of despair. I believe God's grace is trying to flow, but many frustrate or block grace by making the decision to not step forward, let go of the old, and step into the new (Luke 5:38–39). God is trying to prepare and align us to move forward to create a governing body that is mature and responsible. One who will obey God's laws and commands, who prays together, and understands the power and anointing that comes from prayer (Philippians 3:20, 2 Corinthians 5:19–20, Hebrews 5:11–14, James 5:13–16). I want to lift up all of those who are stuck, fearful, and feel like they can't take that step into something new and step away from the old. Today, I declare fear is gone, faith will rise, and courage will move your feet toward the new.

Father, thank You for Your Son Jesus Christ who reconciled the world to Himself. Father, help us to receive the grace You are sending forth, so we will have the courage, strength, and faith to step into the new, not finding comfort in the old. Open our eyes to see that we are ambassadors of Christ. You have given us the authority to defeat the enemy, take hold of the circumstances around us, and walk through to the new. Help us see all the opportunities to gather as one body and pray together. Give us an increase in faith and understanding to see that You are refining, guiding, edifying, and building each one as part of the body of Christ. When we gather, Father, strengthen us as one, to see how we should govern in order to bring Your kingdom to earth and fulfill Your will. In Yeshua's name I pray, Amen!

Reflection Points:

This week, take note of circumstances that arise, and how you stopped to ask God to help you see beyond what your physical eyes see when your emotions may have pushed you to the fires of presumption or waters of despair. Ask God to sharpen your discernment and help you see beyond the physical.

#NEW
WINE

History

He is the radiance of the glory of God and the
exact imprint of his nature, and he upholds the
universe by the word of his power. After making
purification for sins, he sat down at the right hand
of the Majesty on high. (Hebrews 1:3 ESV)

Part of the story about the wedding in Cana confused me. When
Mary told Jesus about the wine, He said, "Woman, what does this
have to do with me? My hour has not yet come." (John 2:4) If His
time had not come, why did He perform the miracle? I began to
look at more verses in John that mention the same thing about His
time, such as John 7:30 and 8:20. But, in John 12, Jesus states, "The
hour has come for the Son of Man to be glorified." (John 12:23
ESV) Then I realized, he wasn't talking about doing the miracle.
He was talking about when He would be crucified, when His blood
would purify us, and when His living water would fill us, so He
could create new wine. So, He paints a beautiful picture of what is
to come. He uses the purification jars of living water to transform
into new wine. In order to transform the water to wine, He had to
change the history of the water! No matter what sins or failures are
in our past, God can remove those and create new wine to fill our
vessels. Ask the Lord to fill your vessel with His wine and purify
your past. If you don't know Jesus, invite Him in today and ask Him
to forgive your sins.

Lord, thank You for being I AM and creating time! Lord, I see
how You work through time, and You will do what is needed in Your
time. I come as an intercessor in faith, and I lift up all Your children
to You, whether they know You personally or not. I ask You to open
their eyes to see that if Jesus can change the history of water and
make it into new wine, then You can remove sin from their past.

Lead them back to Your love today and give Your children new wine! I declare today that sin is forgotten and blotted out by the blood of Jesus Christ! I declare that the children of God rise up and become new wine! Run to the Lord's mercy and grace and let Him heal you! Lord, bless us with an imprint of Your nature, so the radiance of Your glory will shine through us. May Your will be done on earth as in heaven! In Yeshua's name we pray, Amen!

REFLECTION POINTS:

Think of your story—your history, the present, and what you think your future may look like—and thank God for being merciful and full of grace during the times you made bad decisions. Remember how He grew you during those times. Take a quick second to thank Him each day this week for those times.

CARDINAL

Cardinals

…so that we may no longer be children, tossed to and fro by the waves and carried about by every wind of doctrine, by human cunning, by craftiness in deceitful schemes. Rather, speaking the truth in love, we are to grow up in every way into him who is the head, into Christ, from whom the whole body, joined and held together by every joint with which it is equipped, when each part is working properly, makes the body grow so that it builds itself up in love. (Ephesians 4:14–16 ESV)

I have a family of cardinals that came to live in a tree in my backyard earlier this year, and I watched these two cardinals begin to build their family in this tree as they had their first two baby birds. One day, a hawk flew through the yard and grabbed something, then landed on my fence. I could see he had gotten one of the babies. Now cardinals are fiercely protective, and they were frantic when this happened. As the time approached for the remaining baby bird to learn to fly, their senses had been heightened. It seemed like they were even more aggressive than before every time the baby tried. After many falls and attempts to fly, he did! But imagine how hard it is to let your child go so they could learn to survive on their own and fly, and at the same time, that fierce protection wants to just hold them tight and never let go. God feels the same way about us. He wants to protect us from everything, but He knows if He does, we will never grow and mature as Christians. The parents of the baby cardinal were never far, and they were always ready to pick him up when he fell. Like a loving Father, God is always there to pick us up if we fall. This year has had lots of twists and turns and many falls, but I believe God is picking us up and helping us learn to fly.

Lord, thank You for the loving way You guide, nurture, and protect us. Lord, as we begin to fly, help us to grow stronger and more courageous. Provide wisdom and understanding to why we fall and how to keep from falling again. Help us to grow as Your body in Christ and to learn to lean on one another. Teach us to help each other from falling and being tossed around by the waves of human cunning and craftiness of the enemy. Help us to speak in truth through love and grace. Bless You for being such a loving Father. In Yeshua's name I pray, Amen.

Reflection Points:

This week, ask God to show you three people that need this prayer. I will also ask you to take an even bigger step, and pick one of those three, if not all three, to pray this over them in person.

Cover Us

Hear my cry, O God; attend unto my prayer. From the end of the earth will I cry unto thee, when my heart is overwhelmed: Lead me to the rock that is higher than I. For thou hast been a shelter for me, and a strong tower from the enemy. I will abide in thy tabernacle for ever: I will trust in the covert of thy wings. Selah. For thou, O God, hast heard my vows: thou hast given me the heritage of those that fear thy name. Thou wilt prolong the king's life: and his years as many generations. He shall abide before God for ever: O prepare mercy and truth, which may preserve him. So will I sing praise unto thy name for ever, that I may daily perform my vows. (Psalm 61:1–8 KJV)

Cover us

My heart is overcome with ache and hurt.
To my knees, I fall and my hands, I raise,
and I cry, cover us Lord! Cover us! Hover over us!

For I have seen the depravity and loss.
I felt the grief and held the grievance in my hands.
My ground shifts and shakes as I sway and cry.
Will it ever end? Will healing begin? Will revival come?
Oh Lord, cover us! Cover us! Hover over us!

From above I hear a whisper, look up!
See the sun in the sky that covers you in warmth.

See the stars I have placed to blanket you in the dark.
As the moon reflects the sun, I reflect upon you, and cover you
with my love.

Come and I will shelter you with mercy and grace!
I will be a rock that doesn't shake.
I will fill each step with love and grace!
I will anoint you and provide healing!
I am a strong tower during the wait!

Come to me and I will shelter you under my wing.
Lay down your burdens, give me your hurts
and I will give you rest!
Place the pieces of your heart in my hands.
I will mend and weave it back together.
Feel my love and grace begin to fill your heart
and bring revival upon you.

For I have covered you and given you healing!
I hovered over you and lit your path.
Seek my face and I will hover over and bring you peace.
Come under my wing and I will lead you to revival.

Praise you Lord, for you are covering us!
Praise you Lord, for you are hovering over us!
Praise you Lord, for the light you brought to us!
Praise you Lord, for you will bring revival upon us!
Amen!

Reflection Points:

This week, ask God to reveal any areas that are numb, and ask Him to heal those areas. Go to your secret place, seek His face, and let Him cover you in His healing presence.

Bread

Give us this day our daily bread. (Matthew 6:11 ESV)

In Hebrew, bread means "livelihood" and has the root meaning "to fight." Livelihood is how we support our life, but life fights against our livelihood. Why? The thief comes to steal, kill, and destroy. His main objective is to take the "livelihood" out of our lives because Jesus came to give us an abundance of livelihood for our lives (John 10:10-11). How does he do this? He pulls our emotions in all the wrong directions and creates distractions with his lies. Then our faith wavers, because we open the door to doubt, and this is where the enemy runs wild—Doubt! In Hebrew thought, the heart is the seat of emotions, and the stomach is the seat of life. How can we get these to sit together? Slow down, pay attention to the distractions around you, and close those doors. Begin by stepping beyond the idea of "a prayer life" into "a life of prayer." Jesus gave us the best example of how to get our daily bread—through prayer (Matthew 6:8–15). When you commune with God through prayer, worship, or mediating on His word, He will feed you "the bread of life," so you won't go hungry again (John 6:35). So, when the enemy tries to run wild with your emotions, fight back by communing with God, and let Him be the seat you choose to sit in.

Our Father in heaven, hallowed be your name. Your kingdom come, your will be done, on earth as it is in heaven. GIVE US THIS DAY OUR DAILY BREAD, and forgive us our debts, as we also have forgiven our debtors. And lead us not into temptation but deliver us from evil. (Matthew 6:9–13 ESV) (Emphasis added)

Lord, remove the distractions of the enemy, and help us to close the doors to his lies. Father, slow us down so we can see how to shift to a life of prayer, and never miss a moment to come sit and commune with You. To You are the kingdom, the power, and the glory forever. In Yeshua's name I pray, Amen.

Reflections Points:

This week, shift your prayer life. Begin each morning with thirty minutes of prayer or worship, and throughout the day, take five minutes and spend it with God. Thank Him for prayer and ask him to open your heart to a life of prayer.

Gates of Hell

> Now when Jesus came into the district of Caesarea
> Philippi…. And Jesus answered him…. "you are
> Peter, and on this rock I will build my church,
> and the gates of hell shall not prevail against it. I
> will give you the keys of the kingdom of heaven,
> and whatever you bind on earth shall be bound in
> heaven, and whatever you loose on earth shall be
> loosed in heaven." (Matthew 16:13–19 ESV)

In Caesarea Philippi, there was a temple that sat in front of a cave that
was believed to be the gateway to the underworld; this is where the
Greek god Pan lived. This cave's main attraction was for Hellenistic
pagan worship which included strange sexual acts with goats. I
believe Jesus took the disciples to these gates, not only to show His
authority to them, but to show Satan who Jesus will also give this
authority to. He said Peter's confession is the rock on which He will
build His church and the gates of hell shall not prevail! So, Jesus
took His disciples to hell's gate and threw down the gauntlet! If we
are called to be part of God's church, then that same authority is
ours also, right? Yes!

> So then you are no longer strangers and aliens,
> but you are fellow citizens with the saints and
> members of the household of God, built on the
> foundation of the apostles and prophets, Christ
> Jesus himself being the cornerstone, in whom the
> whole structure, being joined together, grows into a
> holy temple in the Lord. In him you also are being
> built together into a dwelling place for God by the
> Spirit. (Ephesians 2:19–22 ESV)

You and I have that same authority, and hell's gates cannot prevail! Brothers and sisters, stand on God's Word and help build God's church in unity and strength. Let's throw the gauntlet down and show some authority!

Father, thank You for Your Son Jesus Christ! Thank You for anointing us with the authority that Jesus took from hell's gates. This physical world is very loud and confusing, and we battle our flesh every day to see past this world into the spiritual. Father, reveal that authority to us today. Help us to see how to use it to build Your church so the gates of hell will never prevail! Unite us together as one body, built on the foundation of the apostles and prophets with Jesus Christ as our cornerstone that joins all of us together as one new man under God, bound by Your love and truth. Anoint us today with boldness and courage and help us walk in Your kingdom authority. Please send Your angels to minister and help us battle in building Your church. In Yeshua's name I pray, Amen.

Reflection Points:

Ask God every day this week to show where you need to use this authority in your life, and how to use the power of His Word to do that.

Fear

When I am afraid, I put my trust in you. (Psalm 56:3 ESV)

Now faith is the assurance of things hoped for, the conviction of things not seen. (Hebrews 11:1 ESV)

Many are gripped with fear—fear of what is to come, fear of sickness, or fear of how they will survive whatever they are going through. One day, I stared fear in the eyes, though it wasn't my own fear. A lady and her daughter flipped over on a float, got caught in the water's current and didn't come back up. All the sudden, I and four others jumped into the water and began swimming to help. The mom popped up holding her teenage daughter but was struggling to swim. Reaching the mom, we tried to take her daughter from her and let her swim, but she wouldn't let go! Finally, exhausted and worn out, she had no option but to let go. The daughter was right in front of me, but she was literally paralyzed by fear. The look in her eyes was terrifying when she stared right at me and then just sank! I remembered being shocked she didn't fight to live! I snapped back to my senses, but all I could see was the last piece of her long hair disappearing completely. I grabbed her hair and pulled her up, swam to a man close to me, and pushed her to him. He then pulled her out of the water. I think about that incident, and how God provided all the help they needed, but they couldn't see past the fear. I want to pray today to break your fear and free you to see that God has provided all you need, but you must trust.

Father, thank You for providing all we need and always giving us a way out through You. Lord, increase our faith so we see past the fear, and open our eyes to see You are the assurance of things hoped for. Help us trust the things we can't see, let go of what is gripping us by fear, and hand it to You. Bless my brothers and sisters with peace and understanding beyond what they see. In Yeshua's name I pray, Amen!

Reflection Points:

What do you fear? What is keeping you from taking that step of faith to trust God in whatever you are facing? This week, every day confess that fear to God, and declare that your fear is broken, and your faith will rise!

#WRESTLE

Wrestle

So Jacob called the name of the place Peniel, saying,
"For I have seen God face to face, and yet my life
has been delivered." (Genesis 32:30 ESV)

Sometimes I find it hard to relate to the people in the Bible
when I try to put myself in their shoes to figure out what they
are feeling. I have thought a lot about Jacob wrestling with God
and wonder what he was truly wrestling with. He had made
a full circle and was back at the place he feared—confronting
Esau. Jacob was soon to face his brother, and he feared his wrath
for stealing Esau's blessing (Genesis 27). He prayed for God to
protect him and reminded God of the promises He made to
Jacob. He praised God's steadfast love, faithfulness, and goodness
and thanked God because he was unworthy (Genesis 32:9-12).
Do you think Jacob wrestled with where God had brought him
back to, or do you think he wrestled with his faith and feeling
worthy enough to step into the role God had for him? There have
been times I have struggled with my faith and self-worth. Many
times, I have questioned something over and over, because I just
couldn't trust where God had placed me and what God wanted
me to do. Like Jacob, I have wrestled, and like Jacob, I won't give
up until I have deliverance. I know God's love is steadfast. He
is faithful, merciful, gracious, slow to anger, and wants good for
me (Exodus 34:6).

Father, thank You for Your love, mercy, and grace. So many
times, I have wrestled with where I am and what I am doing. My trust
waivers, and I question the abilities You placed in me. Abba, please
silence my flesh, still the quiver I feel, and anoint me with peace for
this journey. Replace all the fear with courage and overwhelm my
heart with the presence of Your love. Lord, I lift all my brothers and

sisters up to You and ask You to fill them with Your Presence. Fill them with Your love and place a boldness inside each of them to trust where You have placed them. Raise their faith in the abilities You have placed in each of them. Bless us today by bringing us face to face with You, and deliver us. In Yeshua's name I pray, Amen.

REFLECTION POINTS:

What are you wrestling with? Is God trying to help you overcome a cycle of mistrust and build your courage to trust what He is doing? How is He using you to help fulfill something bigger than what you perceive? Stop wrestling and just let God fill you each day with His presence and build a trusting relationship with Him.

Deeper

And in the fourth watch of the night he came to them, walking on the sea. But when the disciples saw him walking on the sea, they were terrified, and said, "It is a ghost!" and they cried out in fear. But immediately Jesus spoke to them, saying, "Take heart; it is I. Do not be afraid." And Peter answered him, "Lord, if it is you, command me to come to you on the water." He said, "Come." So Peter got out of the boat and walked on the water and came to Jesus. But when he saw the wind, he was afraid, and beginning to sink he cried out, "Lord, save me." Jesus immediately reached out his hand and took hold of him, saying to him, "O you of little faith, why did you doubt?" (Matthew 14:25–31 ESV)

Have you ever wondered why the disciples were so terrified? Had they seen ghosts before walking on water? I asked myself these questions and I realized that Jesus chose the fourth watch to come to them on chaotic waters. Why? That watch is from 3am–6am—the witching hour! This is the time believed to be when satanic activities would occur. He wanted to show them He had authority ALL the time and over the chaotic winds and deep waves. Peter realizes who it is walking on these chaotic waters and says, "Lord, if that is You command me to come to You on the water." (Matthew 14:28) In Hebrew, a command doesn't mean a demand or an order, rather, it means to guide or reveal a path. Peter was saying, "Show me the way, reveal this path to me so I can walk with You anywhere and anytime!" Jesus said "COME." (Matthew 14:29) Peter stepped off and walked to Jesus. What do you think the other disciples were thinking? I think in their minds they were amazed, but they thought he was going to sink because none of them stepped off with him and none of them encouraged him. Could that have hindered his faith a little, caused him to take his eyes off Jesus, and focus on the chaos? How deep does your faith go? Will you step out of the shallow waters and go deeper? Don't look around for someone to cheer you on! Most people think you will sink! Prove them wrong and walk on water!

Lord, thank You for taking us deeper. Lord, strengthen our faith and remove this fear of sinking! Help our eyes to focus only on You! Peter didn't sink! You had him and You have us! Today Lord, I ask You to call Your children deeper! Build their faith to walk on water and not sink! Remove the lies of fear and insecurities and replace it with Your all-consuming love! In Yeshua's name we pray, Amen.

REFLECTION POINTS:

Will you step off into the deep this week? Will you help and encourage others to step out also?

Each day, take a small step off into deeper waters, and ask God to guide you through. Keep your focus on Him and not the people around you.

Stones

…that this may be a sign among you. When your children ask in time to come, 'What do those stones mean to you?' then you shall tell them that the waters of the Jordan were cut off before the ark of the covenant of the Lord. When it passed over the Jordan, the waters of the Jordan were cut off. So these stones shall be to the people of Israel a memorial forever." (Joshua 4:6–7 ESV)

This story in Joshua hit me the other day differently during a women's group I attend. They asked this question: what are the stones of remembrance in your life? For some reason my mom kept coming to my mind, and I started to think about 2020 and how it has been a bitter, bittersweet year for me. I lost my mom on Easter, and our relationship had been strained over the years. Walls and mountains had formed between us. About three or four months before she passed, I called her to try to break some of these walls down. We had just started to really speak again, and I really hoped to try to build a bridge between her and my son, because he didn't know her well and didn't know much about her. Unfortunately, we didn't get to build that bridge, but I have found myself talking about her all the time and sharing memories from the past. So, after the women's group that day, I came home and sat in my living room looking at all the things I acquired when my sister and I moved our mother's belongings. I realized I had placed stones of remembrance all around me and at that moment, I felt her presence. I realized it isn't too late for my son to know her. I can begin to place stones of remembrance around him and begin to build that bridge I wanted to before she passed.

Lord, thank You for Your Word and that it is timeless, and

no matter the times we are going through, Your Word will speak to us. Thank you for the stones of remembrance and the trials we go through. Help me to build a bridge of remembrance for my son. Today bless all relationships and help to build strong bridges between them. Bring children back to parents, and parents back to children, and place stones of remembrance in their lives today. In Yeshua's name I pray, Amen.

Reflection Points:

What are the stones of remembrance in your life? This week, make note of the stones you have placed around you, what those stones mean to you, and how you will carry them into the legacy you are building.

HEART
BROKEN
♥

Heartbroken

I'm heartsick and heartbroken by it all. Their contempt has crushed my soul. I looked for sympathy and compassion but found only empty stares. (Psalm 69:20 TPT)

Every day I ask God to break my heart, because I want to understand God's heart for people. One day, God really broke my heart through a homeless man named Pirate. I met him at a church service that our church had partnered with to feed the homeless. This man had a story that sounded like a movie, and he was pretty broken by life and the people who mistreated him. He was very truthful! Although he believed in God, he said he didn't forgive people and therefore he didn't ask God for forgiveness because he felt he would be a hypocrite. Then he began to talk about his mom and how he wants to see her again, but she won't see him. I asked him why. He said she doesn't want to be sorrowful and so, she has asked him not to come around. I wanted to say so much to him, but I felt I should just listen (James 1:19). Before he left, my son and I said bye and he looked at my son and said, "You make your mom proud, ok?" My son said, "I will." I told him I love my son very much, and there is nothing he could do to take my love away. I know he is a blessing from God, and I will always remember that no matter what happens in life. I know his mom feels this way even though love hurts sometimes. Before he left, I thanked him for letting us talk with him because he blessed my heart. He peeked over his glasses, tilted his head, and said, "Really?" I replied yes, and he said thank you also. Then he was gone. I realized he hadn't had someone just sit and listen to him and show him genuine love. This day my heart broke, because all I wanted to do was fill him with God's Word and hope he felt

God's love and forgiveness. But I was only to plant a small seed that someone else will come along to water and grow!

Lord thank You for breaking my heart and showing me love comes in so many ways! Thank You for showing that sometimes silence is more powerful than words. I lift all families up to You because there is so much division and strife! Lord, fill homes with overwhelming love that heals, repairs, and redeems the family unit. Lord, bring people into all your children's lives that need a seed planted, and grow and nurture those seeds. Bless all families today, Lord, and bring prodigal children home! In Yeshua's name I pray, Amen!

REFLECTION POINTS:

This week, begin planting seeds in people and pray God will nurture and grow those seeds. Ask Him to show you how to help grow and nurture seeds that others may have planted.

Your Story

But, as it is written, "What no eye has seen, nor ear heard, nor the heart of man imagined, what God has prepared for those who love him"— these things God has revealed to us through the Spirit. For the Spirit searches everything, even the depths of God. For who knows a person's thoughts except the spirit of that person, which is in him? So also no one comprehends the thoughts of God except the Spirit of God. (1 Corinthians 2:9–11 ESV)

Have you ever looked back at your history and, all the sudden, events in your past began to connect? You realize you are finally seeing the story God wrote for you beginning to make some sense. It can be exciting and scary at the same time because your mind tries to fill in the blanks and starts to create paths that you see God will go! I did this with a Jehovah's Witness that came to my door one day. On this day, I decided to let them in and listen to them, but of course it wasn't before I stated I am a Christian and I believe in Jesus! She was totally fine with it. For a year and a half, she would come to my house and bring one to two more Jehovah's Witnesses (JW) with her. As they shared the word, I found that they knew more about the Bible than me! I became very jealous of a person that wasn't of my faith and knew more about the Bible than me. I wasn't having this, so I began to study the Word of God and research their religion. I began to understand more and realized the differences in what we believed. Funny thing is, most of the time they came over, we didn't talk a lot about God. We would just visit and talk about what was going on in our lives. But I didn't stop filling up with the Word of God because I wanted to be prepared and ready for battle. Since covid, my JW friends stopped coming over and stopped texting. I felt like I had failed and didn't do the job God gave me, but then I realized it wasn't for them, it was for me! Wow! God knows how to meet you where you are and find a way to reel you back. Amen!

Lord, all I can say is thank You! I bow at Your feet and give You all I have because I know you will mold and shape me to Your glory. I understand that You know how to prepare me for my story, and You know the tools I need to travel this journey. I trust Your plan, purpose, and most of all Lord, I trust my story You have already written for me. Today, Lord, begin to connect the dots for all Your children, show them their story, and bless them with the assurance that You will provide everything they need. In Yeshua's name I pray, Amen!

REFLECTION POINTS:

This week, stop and just thank God every day for your story. Ask Him to build your trust, to let Him reveal your story to you, and continue to walk each day in that trust.

Reckless Love

"And as soon as we heard it, our hearts melted, and there was no spirit left in any man because of you, for the Lord your God, he is God in the heavens above and on the earth beneath. Now then, please swear to me by the Lord that, as I have dealt kindly with you, you also will deal kindly with my father's house, and give me a sure sign that you will save alive my father and mother, my brothers and sisters, and all who belong to them, and deliver our lives from death." (Joshua 2:11–13 ESV)

I was listening to the song "Reckless Love," and I thought, what does that look like? How is God's love reckless? Then I recalled the story of Rahab the prostitute, and how she hid the two spies Joshua sent into Jericho. She decided to help them because she had heard of all the miraculous things that happened with Moses, and she knew "the Lord your God, he is God in the heavens above and on the earth beneath." (Joshua 2:11) She boldly asked the two spies to protect her when the battle occurs and save her and her family. They agree. So, imagine for a minute, how Rahab felt once the spies left. She had to trust that they would keep their word. She obeys and hides in her home with her family. While the battle was going on, what do you think they heard or even thought? Were they scared or did they have doubts? All the sudden, it is over, they are still alive, and the spies are there to take them out of the city. While the destroyed city burned, do you think she looked at the reckless destruction and understood God's love? I do. He has personally torn down walls in my life. He saved my life and I truly understand what reckless love is!

Lord, thank You for Your boundless, reckless love. Thank you for the generations that sacrificed to bring the foundation we need to stand on that love. Lord, tear down the walls, destroy the lies, and reveal Your reckless love today. Bless all Your children, lost or not, with Your heart. Melt their hearts to see Your miraculous love, filling them with trust and hope that You will lead them through the destruction and bring them to You. Bring heaven and earth into alignment. In Yeshua's name I pray, Amen!

REFLECTION POINTS:

This week, thank God for the walls He has already torn down. Ask Him to show walls that still need to come down, so you have room for God to grow you in the season of life you are in.

Table

You prepare a table before me in the presence of my enemies; you anoint my head with oil; my cup overflows. (Psalm 23:5 ESV)

I often have read this verse and tried to understand what it means. I have even asked different people what they think. Then I was reading about Jesus (Yeshua) at Passover, and before He was crucified. He was anointed and He sat at a table with His enemy (Matthew 26). To prepare something for a purpose or use it, is usually planned in advance, working out all the details so the purpose is fulfilled. I believe Jesus is the table prepared for me. Jesus, which is the Word of God that became flesh, is what my table is set with to prepare my way. I was anointed with His blood so I could sit in the presence of our enemies and know I have victory. But what happens to my enemies? Jesus said "...but woe to that man by whom the Son of Man is betrayed! It would have been better for that man if he had not been born" (Matthew 26:24 ESV). I guess you can't have your cake and eat it too (1 Corinthians 10:21). So, as I step into each day, my table is set and prepared for VICTORY, and because I am anointed with Yeshua' s blood, I am protected by the powerful Word of God from my enemies. What is your table set with?

Lord, thank You for the table You have set! Thank you for the anointed blood of Your Son that was poured out on the cross. Thank You for the Word that became flesh. Lord, help me to walk into each day prepared for victory and to know I am protected from my enemies. Lord, anoint all Your children today and lead them to the table You have prepared for them. Help them see they have victory! In Yeshua's name I pray, Amen.

REFLECTION POINTS:

This week, every day declare this over yourself and others who need victory in this season. "I declare the Lord, my God gives me victory and therefore, I will stand steadfast and immovable, continuing to do God's good work, and I know my labors are not in vain! Amen!"

> But thanks be to God, who gives us the victory through our Lord Jesus Christ. Therefore, my beloved brothers, be steadfast, immovable, always abounding in the work of the Lord, knowing that in the Lord your labor is not in vain. (1 Corinthians 15:57–58 ESV)

Altars

"Stay here with the donkey," Abraham told the servants. "The boy and I will travel a little farther. We will worship there, and then we will come right back."; "This is what the Lord says: Because you have obeyed me and have not withheld even your son, your only son, I swear by my own name that I will certainly bless you." (Genesis 22:5,17 NLT)

Worship is an act of surrender or of sacrifice. What do you need to surrender? Insecurities? Selfishness? Pride? Hurt? Unforgiveness? Take it to the altar. He will cover you with His mercies and fill you with His love. He will provide you what you need. Surrender your worship to Him. He sacrificed His life for you.

Lord, thank You for being Jehovah Jireh, our provider! I will surrender all my worship to You! I give my dances and praises as a sacrifice to Your goodness and love at the altar, yielding myself to You and giving all I possess to You. I will not withhold any part of me from You! I will worship You with all I have, for You have shown me Your mercies. You have provided when I was weak! You lifted me up when I fell. You guided me along a lighted path. You sacrificed Your life so I could live! Please take me to the altar, for I surrender all to You! Praise Your mighty name! My tambourine rattles the message, "Praise You Lord...bless Your Son Jesus Christ."

I dance and sing, and I will worship unto Your name, all the days of my life. In Yeshua's name I pray, Amen!

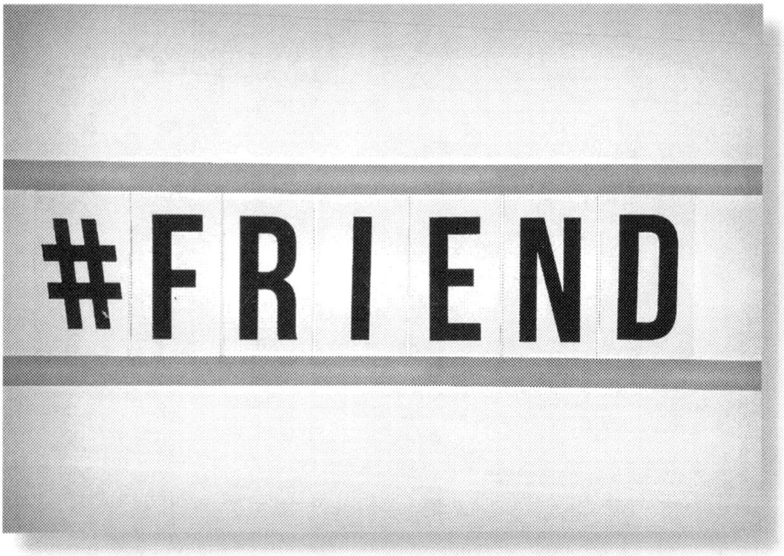
#FRIEND

Friend

And the scripture was fulfilled which saith, Abraham believed God, and it was imputed unto him for righteousness: and he was called the Friend of God. (James 2:23 KJV)

The Lord said, "Shall I hide from Abraham what I am about to do, seeing that Abraham shall surely become a great and mighty nation...For I have chosen him...Abraham what he has promised him." Then the Lord said, "Because the outcry against Sodom and Gomorrah"... Then Abraham drew near and said, "Will you indeed sweep away the righteous with the wicked? ... Suppose ten are found there." He answered, "For the sake of ten I will not destroy it." (Genesis 18:17–32 ESV)

Friendship consists of a few things—association, loyalty, and affection. Abraham was associated with God, was loyal to God, and affectionately loved God. But God was also these things toward Abraham. Before God went to destroy the cities of Sodom and Gomorrah, He wanted to talk with his friend first. Abraham started to intercede and negotiate for the people because his brother and family lived there. Wow! Abraham was negotiating with God! He was appealing to the love and mercy that God had for him and has for all His children, lost or not! God was willing to do what Abraham asked because He saw him as His friend. You and I can have a friendship with God the same way! How? Easy—trust Him in all things. Talk to God about everything. Make it the first thing you do before making any decisions. As a matter of fact, do it before your feet hit the floor in the morning! Say God, I can't do this without You today, please be my friend and walk with me today!

Father, thank You for being our friend. As our Father and friend, please bring all Your children into a friendship with You! Open our eyes to see the love You have for us. Just like Abraham, we can have a friendship in which we can come to You, talk to You, and negotiate our decisions with You. Build our friendship through loyalty and affection and remind us that our association with You came through Your Son, Jesus! Bless Your Son and the price He paid so we could come and be in Your presence. In Yeshua's name I pray, Amen!

REFLECTION POINTS:

Every day I want you to talk to God like He is Your best friend. That means you can yell, cry, or just thank Him for always being there and knowing you better than you know yourself.

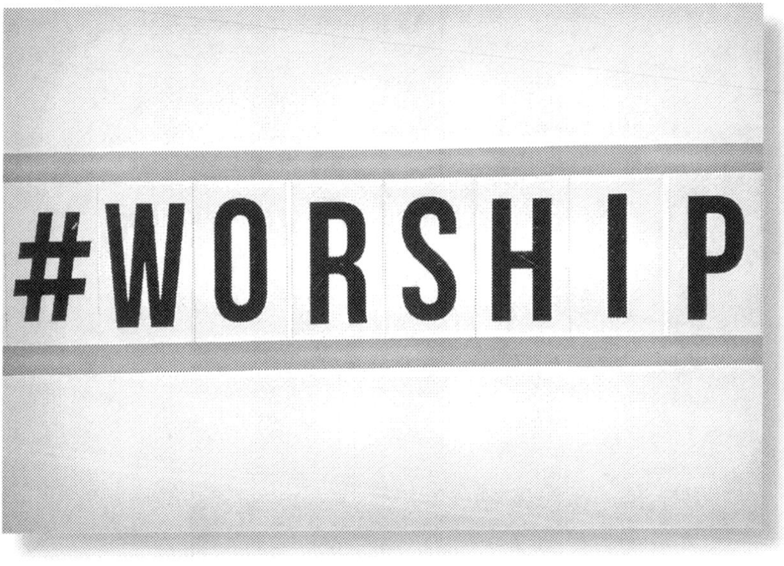
#WORSHIP

Worship

The Lord is my shepherd; I shall not want. He makes me lie down in green pastures. He leads me beside still waters. He restores my soul. He leads me in paths of righteousness for his name's sake. Even though I walk through the valley of the shadow of death, I will fear no evil, for you are with me; your rod and your staff, they comfort me. You prepare a table before me in the presence of my enemies; you anoint my head with oil; my cup overflows. Surely goodness and mercy shall follow me all the days of my life, and I shall dwell in the house of the Lord forever. (Psalm 23:1–6 ESV)

I began to think about David and how the Lord sought out a man after His own heart (1 Samuel 13:14). Do you think God found one? Well, the Bible has sixty-six chapters about David. His bloodline was that of Jesus, and he helped lay the foundation for his son Solomon, to build God's temple (1 Chronicles 28:10–11). I believe David truly knew God's heart because he understood and knew God's will and truly trusted God. Even though he sinned and fell, he learned to lament, get back up, and keep going for God's glory. But I believe he knew something we didn't—how to war with his worship! He would sing, dance, and give all his gratitude to God in low places, on the mountain tops, and in the darkest valleys. He knew God would prepare his table with the supplies and tools he needed to win his battles. What is on the table? The bread of life, the living Word of God! In Hebrew, bread means "livelihood" and contains a root word meaning "to fight." I feel that my livelihood has been a fight lately, and I am weary and surrounded by confusion and chaos. So, today I will worship and fight to keep my livelihood filled with joy, because I know God is all I need, and He only wants goodness for me. He will have mercy on me when I sin, and He will fight and prepare me for the battles. Join me today and worship through this fight and give all your gratitude to your Father, who will provide everything you need.

Father, You are my shepherd (Jehovah Rohi) and You will provide all my needs (Jehovah Jireh). You are my righteousness (Jehovah Tsidkenu) that guides my path and gives me peace (Jehovah Shalom) in dark valleys. You are my abiding presence (Jehovah Shammah) and You have sanctified me (Jehovah M'kaddesh). You have prepared my table with everything I need (El Shaddai). You have covered me with Your anointing, so I walk in the banner of Your victory (Jehovah Nissi). Praise You! I will dance and sing of Your love. I will bow at Your feet and give all my gratitude and love to You. Father, search my heart and make it like Yours! In Yeshua's name, Amen!

Reflection Points:

This week, make note of different worship songs you gravitate to during hard times and during easy times. Make a different playlist of those songs and have them handy when all you need is to just worship and give it to God.

Checkpoint

And I will ask the Father, and he will give you
another Helper, to be with you forever, even the
Spirit of truth, whom the world cannot receive,
because it neither sees him nor knows him. You
know him, for he dwells with you and will be in
you. (John 14:16–17 ESV)

I had a dream several weeks ago that I want to share because I felt this
wasn't just for me. This dream was silent, but I could feel everything
that was being said. I was driving my car to a border checkpoint
and in my passenger seat, was a new comforter, white sheets, and a
pillow. I drove up to the checkpoint where an angel dressed in army
fatigues and holding a clipboard came to my passenger side window.
He looked at his clipboard and then at my passenger seat. While he
was looking at the clipboard, I glanced at a building to the right
which was filled with people who looked frustrated, worried, and
discouraged. Many were going through all their things, checking
to see if they had everything they needed to go forward. They were
questioning every step and their abilities to complete those steps.
When I turned back to the Angel, he pointed forward and I felt this
urgency to go. I hit the gas but then I woke up. We are vehicles that
carry the Holy Spirit through which He provides comfort, guidance,
and security to go forward (1 Corinthians 6:19, 2 Timothy 2:21,
John 14:10–20). I feel God is saying to those who feel like they
can't step forward because they feel deficient, fearful, or insecure,
that vehicles are coming which will help carry you while giving
you comfort, guidance, and security to take those steps forward (2
Kings 4:1–5, Zechariah 4:6). God is building the body of Christ,
and we should be able to come alongside each other and use our
strengths to sharpen and refine one another. While growing and

maturing into vehicles with an abundance of supplies, we should be able to help carry someone else to their destination (Galatians 6:1–10, 2 Corinthians 1:3–7). I feel many are at a checkpoint right now, and I want to be a vehicle of encouragement for you and lift you up in prayer. I hope this will help bring some comfort and give you a secure step to go!

Father, thank You for the Holy Spirit and the guidance and comfort He gives. Prepare us to be vehicles supplied with an abundance of knowledge, compassion, mercy, and grace to pick someone else up along the way and help them prepare their vehicles. Align us as one body in Christ to grow in courage, strength, knowledge, and maturity in order to see when we need to help carry someone and when someone needs to carry us. Father, open all our senses to be able to focus on You and step forward. Help us to trust the abilities You placed in us and move past the checkpoint into something new. Thank You Father, for Your steadfast love and mercy which leads us through and provides all we need. Bless us with unity to fulfill Your will. All this I pray in Yeshua's name, Amen.

REFLECTION POINTS:

This week, ask the Holy Spirit to reveal to you what the next step is—whether it is being a vehicle for someone or asking for a vehicle to come along for you. Once you know which, GO!

Church

I have been asking God what building His church looks like and how I can help build it.

In Ephesians 2:22, it says Jesus is our cornerstone and in Him, we are being built together by the Holy Spirit into a dwelling place for God. If we go back to Genesis 10, Noah's descendants were called the table of nations, and the next chapter is Babel. I realized God created diversity and culture at the Tower of Babel through the table of nations. I feel like if I am going to mature and grow into the body of Christ, then I should learn more about other cultures and begin to celebrate the diversity within all the nations of God. This is how we should begin to sharpen each other through our differences. It will mature us and grow us together to be a body built on Christ for the Kingdom of God. James 5 says to confess your sins to one another and pray for one another. I want to confess to you that I have prejudice towards other cultures and have closed myself off to understanding the differences and learning to respect, grow, and love those diversities. I ask for forgiveness from you today, and I believe we should challenge one another not just to confess our sins but be almost like a check and balance system for each other to grow and mature from one another. "Those whom I love, I reprove and discipline, so be zealous and repent. Behold, I stand at the door and knock. If anyone hears my voice and opens the door." (Revelation 3:14-22 ESV). Jesus is standing at the door of His church waiting for us to open and let Him build us into one body founded on the foundation He built from all tribes, peoples, and languages (Revelation 7:9-10). I want to mature and grow so I have been challenged to pray with people who are diverse from me and to learn more about other cultures and languages.

When I was a child, I spoke like a child, I thought like a child, I reasoned like a child. When I became a man, I gave up childish ways. For now we see in a mirror dimly, but then face to face. Now I know in part; then I shall know fully, even as I have been fully known. So now faith, hope, and love abide, these three; but the greatest of these is love.

(1 Corinthians 13:11–13 ESV)

Father, thank You for building us together as your church and giving Your Son as the cornerstone that holds it together. Father, help us put childish things down and mature us into men and women filled with Your presence who are willing to sit down and learn from someone who is different from us. Grow our maturity through faith, hope, and love so we begin to see past the dimly lit mirror and come face to face with You. Father, bless You for the table of nations and the different tribes, tongues, and peoples You created to build Your church. In Yeshua's name I pray, Amen.

REFLECTION POINTS:

I challenge you this week to step out, reach out to someone who is different from you, and get to know them. Begin to sharpen one another by respecting one another's differences.

Atonement

So if our sins have been forgiven and forgotten, why would we ever need to offer another sacrifice for sin? And now we are brothers and sisters in God's family because of the blood of Jesus, and he welcomes us to come into the most holy sanctuary in the heavenly realm—boldly and without hesitation. For he has dedicated a new, life-giving way for us to approach God. For just as the veil was torn in two, Jesus' body was torn open to give us free and fresh access to him! (Hebrews 10:18–20 TPT)

Yom Kippur or the Day of Atonement is the day the high priest would go behind the veil into the Holy of Holies and offer a sacrifice on the mercy seat to atone for the sins of Israel (Leviticus 16). Another goat called a "scapegoat" was released into the wilderness as a symbol of something bearing the sins and taking them away. Christ bore our sins just as the scapegoat bore the sins of the Israelites. He was blameless and died so our sins can be forgiven, and He asks us to forgive each other as well. What sins do you need to let go and who do you need to forgive?

Lord, I approach Your throne and I bow down and give all my gratitude to Your Son who died for a sinner like me. He made a way to enter Your sanctuary, come to the mercy seat, and say forgive me Abba Father! Forgive me for words that I have spoken that have caused strife and division! Forgive me for the unspoken words and times I chose to remain silent when I should have stood for You! Forgive my actions that have been against Your Word and against the laws You established. Lord, you have shown forgiveness to me, and You ask me to forgive others. So, I too will show forgiveness to others and be a light to Your path of forgiveness. Lord, please show forgiveness upon this nation and all who dwell within this nation. We have failed to keep You as the foundation, and we have allowed man to make our laws instead of abiding in Your laws! Cover us today with Your atonement, show mercy on us, and bring revival upon us! May Your will be done here as in heaven. In Yeshua's name we pray, Amen!

REFLECTION POINTS:

This week, I ask you to reflect on those two questions and seek forgiveness not just for yourself but forgive others as well. Go to a trusted friend who loves Christ and confess your sins to them.

Ask them to pray for you and to hold you accountable. If you are a trusted friend, lend your ear with compassion and open your heart to them without judgement. Be willing to help hold them accountable while showing mercy and grace.

Sukkot

One thing I have desired of the Lord, that I will seek after; that I may dwell in the house of the Lord all the days of my life, to behold the beauty of the Lord, and to enquire in his temple. For in the time of trouble he shall hide me in his pavilion: in the secret of his tabernacle shall he hide me; he shall set me up upon a rock. And now shall my head be lifted up, above mine enemies round about me: Therefore will I offer in his tabernacle sacrifices of joy; I will sing, yea, I will sing praises unto the Lord. (Psalm 27:4–6 KJV)

Sukkot is a festival celebrated in the Bible and is still celebrated as part of Judaism. Sukkot means tabernacle, shelter, booth, or tent. This festival is a commandment of God found in Leviticus 23. As part of the festival, they build a sukkah to remind them of the covering that God provided for the Israelites in the wilderness. I asked some of my friends, who observe this festival, what building the sukkah means to them. They pointed out that the process of building the Sukkah is very important—what you put into your dwelling and how you build your dwelling—because this is what covers you and where you find rest! This is important because if your dwelling shakes or goes through a storm, it needs to be on a good secure foundation and cover you and give you rest no matter what season you are in.

Lord, thank You for covering us! You will never leave us or forsake us! You cover us in trouble and in celebration. Lord, secure our dwellings today with Your presence, cover us, and bring us restoration and revival! In Yeshua's name I pray, Amen.

REFLECTION POINTS:

How have you built your dwelling? Is it secure and on a good foundation? Do you find rest within your dwelling knowing you are covered in God protection? This week, answer these questions and ask God to show you where you could strengthen or rebuild.

Pull Up

I was praying for some friends recently and I had a vision. I was standing in front of a man stuck in a squatting position with a bar full of weights across his shoulders. As I looked closer, it was words that took the shape of weights that weighed him down. Words of discouragement, despair, and cursed words others had spoken over him, and he had spoken over himself. Suddenly, a hand comes down from above and lifts the weight off, and I hear, "Pull Up." I remember thinking, pull up? Why not push up? Then I realized if you are already in a squatting position, it can be hard to get up. Sometimes, you need to pull up on something to help you get stable enough to get back up. The key word is you. God has removed the heavy weights and it is time for YOU to PULL UP! The enemy has convinced you the weight is still there, but it isn't! How do you pull up? Start by pulling down these strongholds of warped ideas, cursed words, and discouraging imaginations. Then use God's Word to pull up by maturing, growing, and sharpening your discernment. But to sharpen your discernment, you must learn how to grow and mature when weight is applied. Your discernment will begin to help you see how to cast down the lies and twisted thoughts that have weighed you down before. This is something I do every time I have a thought not of God. I don't come in agreement with it by repeating it out loud! Then I declared out loud, "I am pulling up and I stand on Your Word Lord!" Your words have power, and you can choose life or death. So, begin today by choosing life, and pull up on God's word (Proverbs 18:21).

> The world is unprincipled. It's dog-eat-dog out there! The world doesn't fight fair. But we don't live or fight our battles that way—never have and never will. The tools of our trade aren't for marketing or

manipulation, but they are for demolishing that entire massively corrupt culture. We use our powerful God-tools for smashing warped philosophies, tearing down barriers erected against the truth of God, fitting every loose thought and emotion and impulse into the structure of life shaped by Christ. Our tools are ready at hand for clearing the ground of every obstruction and building lives of obedience into maturity. (2 Corinthians 10:3–6 MSG)

Father, thank You for providing all the tools we need in Your Word! Thank You for Your Son, Jesus Christ, who took this weight and removed it. Help us mature into a structure shaped by Christ, with tools ready at hand to clear and cast down warped philosophies and tear down anything against God's truth. Guide us through these battles and help our eyes to see and ears to hear You and how You need us to fight these battles. Brothers and sisters, stand with me and declare we are pulling up, and standing on the Word of God, we will pull down the strongholds the enemy has created. Thank You Father for providing all we need to walk in Victory! Sweep a revival of harvest through all Your nations. In Yeshua's name I pray, Amen.

REFLECTION POINTS:

This week, every day choose life and begin to speak blessing over yourself and over others. Declare every morning that you stand on God's Word, and that you will always pull up on His word and pull down the stronghold of lies the enemy has created.

Horizon View

And God said, "Let there be a firmament in the midst of the waters, and let it divide the waters from the waters"... And God called the firmament Heaven..."and let the dry land appear"; and it was so. And God called the dry land Earth...and God saw that it was good. (Genesis 1:6–10 NKJV)

The Space Between

Lord lay me where heaven kisses earth.
Blanket me with rest for my weary soul.
Renew my flesh for the road is long
and give me strength to climb the valleys below.

Lord lift me up in the space between
Where the waters of heaven parted
and show the wisdom that is unknown to me.

Lord speak upon me the words
woven between heaven and earth.
Weave me tightly in the space between
so I stay close to the words You speak to me.

Lord take me on the winds to heaven.
Lift me above the clouds.
Swirl me through the stars
and set my gaze from above
so I look below and praise You.

Lord, hover over me
so Your reflection is all I see.
Breathe into me Your spirit
so I can move in the space
that You weaved into me.

Amen! Praise You Lord! Hallelujah!

REFLECTION POINTS:

Each morning, before you step out of bed ask God to hover over you and breathe a new breath of revival into your heart.

Woman at the Well

The woman left her water jar beside the well and ran back to the village, telling everyone, "Come and see a man who told me everything I ever did! Could he possibly be the Messiah?" So the people came streaming from the village to see him. (John 4:28–30 NLT)

Jacob's well is also believed to be an altar that Jacob built. At this point in Jacob's life, he had wrestled with God, had been given a new name—Israel, and had made peace with his brother. He called this altar El-Elohe-Israel, which means God is the God of Israel (Genesis 33:19-20). So, Jesus, the God of Israel, meets a Samaritan woman at El-Elohe-Israel or Jacob's well, and begins to cross radical barriers of all kinds by choosing a woman to bless. How does He bless her? He chooses her to be the first to announce to everyone who He was—the Messiah! Not only that, when she realizes who He is, she runs away and leaves her jar behind! Why? Because her thirst was quenched. The altar came to her to draw out all the stagnant water and fill her with rivers of living waters (John 7:37-38). Let Jesus fill you today with living water.

Lord, thank You for rivers of living water! Thank You for Your Son who is living water! Lord, I lift all Your children up today who are filled with the stagnant water of this world and ask You to fill them with rivers of living water! Help them to let go of the jar and run to You and be filled! For anyone who is thirsty, come and drink of Jesus and thirst no more! In Yeshua's name I pray, Amen!

REFLECTION POINTS:

This week at bedtime, as you close your eyes, thank God for slumber to your body and sleep for your eyes. Ask Him to remove all the stagnant water that you picked up from the world that day, and fill you with His refreshing, living water so you can go out and conquer the next day.

Dance and Sing

Sing a new song to the Lord, for he has done wonderful deeds. His right hand has won a mighty victory; his holy arm has shown his saving power! The Lord has announced his victory and has revealed his righteousness to every nation! He has remembered his promise to love and be faithful to Israel. The ends of the earth have seen the victory of our God. Shout to the Lord, all the earth; break out in praise and sing for joy! Sing your praise to the Lord with the harp, with the harp and melodious song, with trumpets and the sound of the ram's horn. Make a joyful symphony before the Lord, the King! (Psalm 98:1-6 NLT)

Today, break out in song and dance unto the Lord! He is the Prince of Peace, the God of love, and He never loses! Sing because you LOVE Him and because He LOVES you!

Lord, I call You mighty warrior! Prince of peace! Lord, I sing of Your love and mercy! You remember Your promises! Praise You Lord! You are faithful! You are love! You are our savior!

Your righteousness has been revealed to all nations! I will sing for joy! I will break out into song and dance! My trumpet blows for Your unfailing love! My tambourine rattles, "Lord You are King!" My feet dance with the joyful noise before You Lord! You are King of Kings, Lord of Lords, Prince of Peace! And I will sing of Your goodness and love forever! Amen!

REFLECTION POINTS:

Find some time this week to put on a worship song that makes you want to get up, dance around, and give praises to God.

Be Light

This little light of mine
I'm going to let it shine
Let it shine, all the time, let it shine
All around the neighborhood
I'm going to let it shine
Hide it under a bushel? No!
I'm going to let it shine
Don't let Satan [blow] it out!
I'm going to let it shine
Let it shine, all the time, let it shine

By John Lomax

"You are the light of the world. A city set on a hill cannot be hidden. Nor do people light a lamp and put it under a basket, but on a stand, and it gives light to all in the house. In the same way, let your light shine before others, so that they may see your good works and give glory to your Father who is in heaven." (Matthew 5:14–16 ESV)

This little light of mine used to not shine. It wasn't but a few years ago that my light almost went out. I was part of the opiate crisis and had become an addict and was very ill for many years. I remember, I hated to open the blinds and let the sun in. I was more comfortable sitting in the dark away from the light. My world was always dark, but one day it became completely engulfed in darkness. I was very ill, worn out, and so tired that I was at the point of taking my own life. I sat one night debating this, crying out to God, and asking Him why. Where was He? What did I do to get to this point? I remember hearing a voice say, "I am here!" I said, "I need help, I love my family, but they don't need me, and I can't do this anymore." I clearly heard Him say, "Trust me and take my hand." I looked up and a vision of a hand reaching down came to my mind's eye, and I stood up and said, "Okay." All the sudden, I could see my light was switched on and I had this warm feeling come over me. Everything seemed different and it seemed like it was going to be okay. My perspective began to change, and I could see that my eyes had been closed to light. Once I turned the light on, I could see that light doesn't have to fight the darkness, but darkness flees from light! So, now I open the blinds every day and let the light in. and I try every day to let my light shine for others. I thank God every day for showing me the light!

Lord, thank You for Your light! Thank You for showing me the light. Help me Lord, to be light! Help me to shine my light and make the darkness flee! Use me to show others the light and help them to turn their light on today. Bless all Your children today with Your overwhelming love to light their path and help turn the light on! In Yeshua's name I pray, Amen!

Reflection Points:

Let your light shine every day. Share your story, bless someone, or serve someone this week. Let your light shine while you show and share what God's love is to others.

#ONE
FLESH

One Flesh

And the rib that the Lord God had taken from the man he made into a woman and brought her to the man. Then the man said, "This at last is bone of my bones and flesh of my flesh; she shall be called Woman, because she was taken out of Man."

(Genesis 2:22–23 ESV)

On the last day of April 2020, my husband came back from riding bikes at the bike park with a broken collar bone on his right side. However, two weeks before, I had torn my MCL in my right knee and was immobile. So, we jumped in the car, and my husband said he would drive because he wanted to make it to the hospital. I admit I didn't disagree because I am not the best driver. We get into the car and realize we are both disabled! I can't drive because my right leg is not working well, and he can't start the car or move the gear shift because his right arm isn't working. He looks at me and says, "Well this isn't going to work." I look right at him and turn the key to start the car and put it in reverse. He pulled out and I put it in drive, and he drove to the ER. When we walked in, with his arm tied up with a bed sheet and me on crutches, the receptionist said, "You look like a pair! Who are we helping first?" I laughed so hard! Later, we looked back at that day and realized we didn't miss a beat in figuring out what needed to be done, and we acted as one flesh and worked together. Even though it is a funny story, we grew and learned more about one another during this time, and we learned how to lean on each other in ways we hadn't before. So, I want to pray and lift all marriages up today and ask for growth and strengthening into one flesh!

Father, thank You for marriage and the love You grow between a man and a woman. Lord, today bind husbands and wives together and grow the love they have between one another. Reveal to them today how cherished marriage is to You and how You need to be the center of every marriage. Strengthen the bond between husbands and wives, and bless them with Your grace, mercy, and love. Father, grow them together as one flesh and help them to move and flow as one. In Yeshua's name I pray, Amen.

REFLECTION POINTS:

This week, pray each day for marriages. Pray for your own, someone else's, or your future marriage.

Veteran's Day

And the men said to her, "Our life for yours even to death! If you do not tell this business of ours, then when the Lord gives us the land we will deal kindly and faithfully with you."

(Joshua 2:14 ESV)

This verse always made me stop and think. "Our life for yours even to death." That is a profound statement and although this is easy to say, it isn't easy to understand. I tried to picture a time I would have to literally lay down my life for someone and really, I couldn't, but I realized why! Someone else went before me and fought for my freedom. Many laid down their lives so people like me would not have to make a choice like that. They fought, served, and many died for a purpose that they saw bigger than themselves. They truly understood the verse, "Our life for yours even to death." Today, I want to honor all veterans and thank them for the service they gave and the willingness to lay their life down for mine!

Lord, I lift all veterans to You today. I pray that You place a special favor and blessing upon these men and women that chose to lay their lives down for others and fight for our freedom. Bless them today with peace and fill their hearts with Your overwhelming love. In Yeshua's name I pray, Amen.

REFLECTION POINTS:

This week, thank at least three people who served or are serving in our armed forces.

#ARMOR

Armor

I prayed for a young lady one day and an image kept playing over and over in my mind. I want to share because I felt this was for everyone. I saw a woman in a boxing ring, and she was trying to get a step ahead of her opponent, but she just didn't seem to get there. But suddenly, she was winning by a landslide. At that moment, I felt the Lord say I AM Jehovah Jireh, her provider, and I AM Jehovah Nissi, her banner, and I will fill her vessel with My presence and fight her battles. Then, I was reminded to always put on our armor (Ephesians 6) and that we have angels to assist us.

> For he will command his angels concerning you to guard you in all your ways. On their hands they will bear you up, lest you strike your foot against a stone. You will tread on the lion and the adder; the young lion and the serpent you will trample underfoot. (Psalm 91:11–13 ESV)

This is how I imagine putting my armor on. I start with putting my boots of peace on, and when I slip those on, my angel that God assigned to me, stands behind me and tightens my boots securely to my feet and legs. I pick up my breastplate of righteousness and slide it over my head. Once it sits on my shoulders, my angel tightens the straps on my shoulders and around my waist. He helps me align my belt of truth with the Word of God. When I pick up my sword and slide it into the sheath, it lights up with the written Word of God. Lastly, I pick up my helmet and place it on my head. Once that helmet of salvation touches my head, my angel fastens himself to me. As I pick up my shield of faith, I imagine myself as a mighty warrior of God when I pray.

Father, thank You for fighting our battles, for the armor You have provided and angels You have placed beside us. Praise You, for You are Jehovah-Jireh and Jehovah-Nissi! Fill our vessel with Your spirit so we see the spiritual battle. Secure our amour each day for battle, show us how to prepare for our battles through Your Word, and reveal the power that Your spoken Word holds. Father, help us to be a mouthpiece that speaks power into the airways, helps shift the atmosphere, and breaks the stronghold the enemy has in these battles. Build our trust through these battles so we have the peace to rest in You, because we aren't fighting towards victory, we are fighting from victory! Thank You for being our banner of victory and providing all we need. May your kingdom come, and Your will be done on earth as in heaven. In Yeshua's name I pray, Amen!

Reflection Points:

This week, before you start each day, ask your angel to help you secure your armor. Remember that the battles aren't with the flesh, but spirits and principalities.

Thanksgiving

Acknowledge that the Lord is God! He made us, and we are his. We are his people, the sheep of his pasture. Enter his gates with thanksgiving; go into his courts with praise. Give thanks to him and praise his name. For the Lord is good. His unfailing love continues forever, and his faithfulness continues to each generation. (Psalm 100:3–5 NLT)

We all know the story of Thanksgiving and the pilgrims arriving on the Mayflower at Plymouth Rock. They were greeted by a tribe of Native Americans, who eventually taught the Pilgrims how to cultivate the land. In November of 1621, the pilgrims had their first corn harvest and wanted to show their thanks. So, they planned a festival celebration of the harvest with the Native American tribe. In 1863, during the Civil War, Abraham Lincoln declared Thanksgiving as an official holiday. He gave a touching declaration speech to commemorate the day.

"As a day of Thanksgiving and Praise to our beneficent Father who dwelleth in the Heavens. And I recommend to them that while offering up the ascriptions justly due to Him for such singular deliverances and blessings, they do also, with humble penitence for our national perverseness and disobedience, commend to His tender care all those who have become widows, orphans, mourners or sufferers in the lamentable civil strife in which we are unavoidably engaged, and fervently implore the interposition of the Almighty Hand to heal the wounds of the nation and to restore it as soon as may be consistent with the Divine purposes to the full enjoyment of peace, harmony, tranquility and Union."

Lord, thank You for placing a divine purpose on America—this land where You blessed us and where many from Your tribes and tongues gather together to give You thanks. We praise You because You are good, Your love never fails, and Your faithfulness will always endure each generation. Lord, I ask for peace, harmony, tranquility, and most of all, unity. Bring healing through our land and comfort to all who are sick, hurting, and lost. I ask You to bless them today and bring gladness to their heart! Lord, You made us and we are Yours! We give You all our praise as we enter into Your courts with thanksgiving, knowing You are good, and You have blessed this land and Your sheep within! In Yeshua's name I pray, Amen!

REFLECTION POINTS:

Give thanks this week to God for His many blessings.

Hanukkah

At that time the Feast of Dedication took place at
Jerusalem. It was winter, and Jesus was walking in
the temple, in the colonnade of Solomon. (John
10:22–23 ESV)

Now upon the same day that the strangers profaned
the temple, on the very same day it was cleansed
again, even the five and twentieth day of the same
month, which is Chislev. And they kept the eight
days with gladness, as in the feast of the tabernacles,
remembering that not long before they had held the
feast of the tabernacles, when as they wandered in
the mountains and dens like beasts. (2 Maccabees
10:5–6 KJVAAE)

I have felt led to research some of the Jewish traditions and why they
celebrate them. When I discovered what Hanukkah was about and
its meaning, I was very moved. Back in 168 BC, King Antiochus
IV outlawed Jewish practice and defiled the Jewish temple, placing
an altar to Zeus there. A small army of Jews called the Maccabees
(in Hebrew means hammer) stood up against the king and fought
to gain their religious freedom and temple back. The vision Daniel
has in chapter 8 is about this battle that took place many years later.
When they went to clean and make the temple holy again, they
discovered they only had enough oil to burn in the menorah for
one day, but God delivered a miracle and it burned for 8 days while
new oil could be prepared. For believers, Hanukkah is a celebration
of God's miracles and the light He brought into this world through
His Son. Hanukkah in Hebrew means dedication and is also called
Feast of Dedication, Festival of Lights, or Feast of the Maccabees.

So, we as a family have decided to celebrate Hanukkah along with Christmas to remember the birth of Christ and to celebrate the light He brings into this world.

Blessed are you, Lord our God, King of the universe, who sets us apart by His commandments and commands us to light the lights of Hanukkah. Blessed are you, Lord our God, King of the universe, who has performed miracles for our fathers in those days at this time. Blessed are you, Lord our God, King of the universe, who has kept us alive and sustained us and enabled us to reach the season. Blessed is Your Son Yeshua, for He is the light You brought in this world. Amen!

REFLECTION POINTS:

I want to challenge you to do your own research into Hanukkah and other Jewish celebrations and see how every one of them is about Yeshua (Jesus).

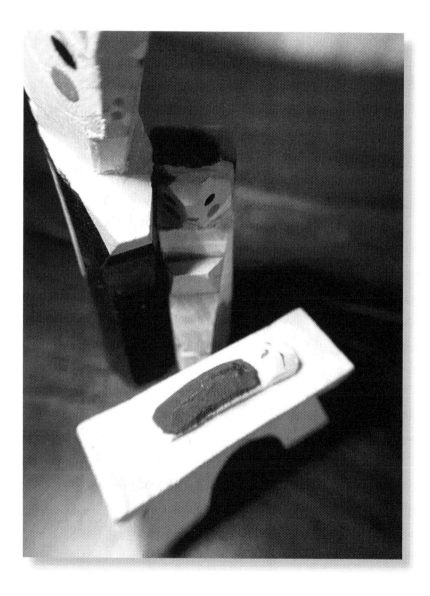

Bethlehem

But you, O Bethlehem Ephrathah, who are too little to be among the clans of Judah, from you shall come forth for me one who is to be ruler in Israel, whose coming forth is from of old, from ancient days. Therefore he shall give them up until the time when she who is in labor has given birth; then the rest of his brothers shall return to the people of Israel. And he shall stand and shepherd his flock in the strength of the Lord, in the majesty of the name of the Lord his God. And they shall dwell secure, for now he shall be great to the ends of the earth. (Micah 5:2–4 ESV)

As I was reading about the birth of Jesus, I wanted to learn what the word Bethlehem means. I know God has a meaning for everything, such as the swaddling cloth, the manger, the star, the shepherds, and the wise men. So, I learned the Hebrew alphabet has twenty-two letters and each letter also represents a number and a picture. This language is very expressive, and I hope one day I will understand it more. According to a website called "The Living Word," Bethlehem, is broken down in Hebrew by the picture and number for each letter. The pictorial meaning states *the Son of God to work a mighty deed (and) to seal a covenant by the sign of the Cross (and) to have authority to provide a sanctuary of safety (and to be) living water.* The numerical meaning breaks down to mean *God the Son, ordinal perfection (at a) divinely perfect period of time (became the) blood sacrifice of Messiah (to give) eternity, new creation (and) new birth (through) testing resulting in revival and resurrection.* Wow! Every detail about Jesus from birth to death has a significant meaning and bears hope for what is to come on the Lord's Day. Amen!

Lord, thank You for the perfect sacrifice You gave us because You love us. Thank You for laying down Your divinity and becoming flesh. Truly, You are God with us—Emmanuel! I glorify and worship unto You and give You all my praises. I sacrifice all I have to You because You sacrificed for me. I will bow and sing, "You are the light of the world, Behold Emmanuel, Behold Messiah, King of Kings and Lord of Lords! Glory be unto Yeshua!

Reflection Points:

This week I want to challenge you to dive deeper and discover all the wonderful mysteries of God's word.

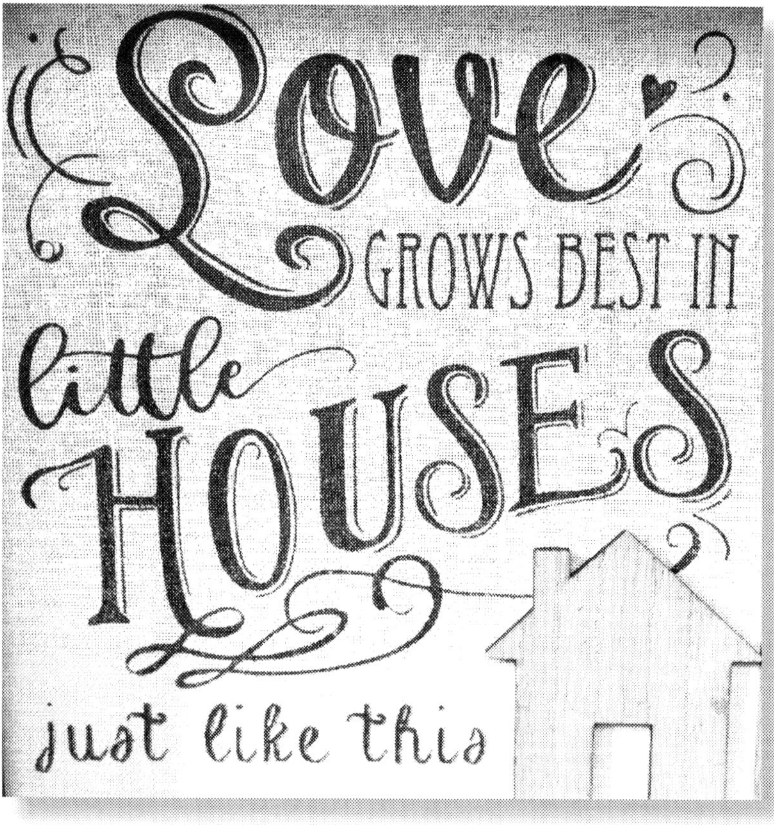
Love
GROWS BEST IN
little
HOUSES
just like this

Mary

For God's temple is holy, and you are that temple.
(1 Corinthians 3:17 ESV)

Luke 2:19 says, "But Mary treasured up all these things, pondering them in her heart." This reminded me of a song by Mark Lowry I really love, "Mary Did You Know?" Every time I listen to it, I am so moved. I wonder if Mary knew her womb was a dwelling place, protecting and covering our Savior, the great I AM. Do you think she realized she was a temple that held the presence of God? Womb in Hebrew means compassion, mercy, and protection from harm. Mary sings praises to the Lord "for he who is mighty has done great things for me, and holy is his name." (Luke 1:46–50 ESV) Why? Because before she could tell Elizabeth she was with child, Elizabeth knew. "And when Elizabeth heard the greeting of Mary, the baby leaped in her womb. And Elizabeth was filled with the Holy Spirit, and she exclaimed with a loud cry, 'Blessed are you among women, and blessed is the fruit of your womb!'" (Luke 1:41–42 ESV) To me, this is a beautiful picture of what God is to us. He wants to dwell within us to protect us, to provide mercy and compassion, and to nurture and grow our spirit. How God wants to use each one of us to be a vessel filled with His spirit to produce blessed fruit.

Lord, thank You for Your Son and for Your Spirit. Lord, empty my vessel, fill it with Your Spirit, dwell within me, and help me grow. Nurture and strengthen me through Your mercy and compassion and help me to produce fruit blessed by You. Lord, grace all Your children today with Your presence and fill their vessel with Your mercy and compassion. In Yeshua's name I pray, Amen.

REFLECTION POINTS:

This week, take some time to listen to the song "Mary Did You Know?" and think about how God wants to dwell within you to fulfill your purpose in His kingdom. Ask Him to prepare your dwelling for His presence to live.

#SHADOW

Shadow

He who dwells in the shelter of the Most High will abide in the SHADOW of the Almighty. I will say to the Lord, "My refuge and my fortress, my God, in whom I trust." For he will deliver you from the SNARE of the fowler and from the deadly pestilence. He will cover you with his pinions, and under his wings you will find refuge; his faithfulness is a SHIELD and buckler. (Psalm 91:1–4 ESV) (emphasis added)

I want to tell you about a dream I had that has stuck with me for several days because I think it might encourage some of you going into this new year. In the dream, I was walking through a desert and the sun was bright and it was hot. I was carrying a full-length mirror in front of me like a shield and it was giving me shade. All the sudden, a huge bright green cobra flared his head like he was going to strike the mirror. For some reason, I got into a fighter stance, gripped my shield tightly, and BAM, he hit the mirror! I would rock back and forth but I didn't fall over because my stance was strong. The snake would shake his head back and forth and then he would strike the mirror again! Then I woke up, and suddenly Psalm 91 popped in my head. Today, I want to pray for everyone and encourage you to take a strong stance in the new year. Abide in the shadow of the Almighty no matter what tries to strike you, and know God is Your refuge and shield. Last year was a roller coaster ride that I didn't enjoy the whole time, and if this year is going to be another ride, then I am going to find a way to hold on and enjoy it.

Lord, thank You for being our refuge and shield. Thank You for protecting us from the snares of the enemies. Help us to abide in Your strength so we can maintain a strong stance. Secure our grip to

Your protecting shield and comfort us in the shadow of Your wings. Lord, guide us through whatever this year brings, and help us find joy and gratitude in low parts, as well as the high parts! We give all the praise and honor to You because You have delivered us, and we are not walking to victory, but we are walking IN victory! In Yeshua's name I pray, Amen.

REFLECTION POINTS:

Meditate on Psalm 91 this week and ask God to cover you in His shadow, strengthen your stance for any strikes that you may encounter, and ask your angel to come and assist you every day.

Printed in the United States
by Baker & Taylor Publisher Services